THE HOCKEY QUIZ BOOK

The Best Humorous, Challenging & Weird Questions & Answers

J. Alexander Poulton

OVER TIME BOOKS

The Publisher: OverTime Books is an imprint of Éditions de la Montagne Verte

Library and Archives Canada Cataloguing in Publication

Poulton, J. Alexander (Jay Alexander), 1977–
      The hockey quiz book : the best humorous, challenging & weird questions & answers / J. Alexander Poulton.

Includes bibliographical references.
      ISBN-13: 978-1-897277-31-7
      ISBN-10: 1-897277-31-8

      1. National Hockey League—Miscellanea. 2. Hockey—Miscellanea. I. Title.

GV847.8.N3P69 2008   796.962'64   C2008-901681-5

Project Director: J. Alexander Poulton
Project Editor: Kathy van Denderen
Production: Jodene Draven
Cover Image: Courtesy of photos.com

We acknowledge the financial support of the Government of Canada through the Book Publishing Industry Development Program for our publishing activities.

PC: P5

Canadian Heritage   Patrimoine canadien

Contents

Dedication

To my Myszka.

Introduction

From the frozen ponds of rural Canada to the ice arenas of the world, the popularity of the game of hockey keeps growing with each passing year. For people like you, dear reader, and myself, each year that goes by means new accomplishments, broken records, strange stories and a million other little bits of information that we get to add to our continually growing arsenal of hockey knowledge. But how much do you really know about the game? From hockey's first baby steps in the 1800s to today's modern game filled with stats, how do you think you might fair in a test of your hockey knowledge? This book is for two kinds of hockey fans. Those who want to know more about the game and those who think they know everything about the game. Every turn of the page lists questions that test your knowledge of the game, and answers are provided that will both surprise and entertain you.

This book is filled with questions that you might know the answers to, while others will leave you scratching your head. Test your knowledge of the game in an entertaining way, and gain some new information at the same time. Whether you are young or old, there is something for everyone in this book. The book is divided into 10 different categories, from Hockey's Humble Origins to the Experts' Corner. Along the way you will be tested on your knowledge of the goaltenders of the game, see what you know about the blue liners, discover new information about your favourite teams and learn a thing or two about some of the lighter moments in the history of the game.

After writing 10 books on hockey, I have come across some interesting facts about the game that the average fan, even the fanatic one, might have never heard about. Things such as finding out who the first player was to take the Stanley Cup to Europe, and who was brave enough to rip Bobby Hull's toupee from his head in the middle of a game. I also discovered some famous hockey quotations said by some famous people, some of whom you might know and some that might surprise.

Chapter One

Hockey's Humble Origins

1. Although widely disputed, where did the first official hockey game take place?

A. Kingston

B. Montréal

C. Halifax

D. Netherlands

2. Who once scored 14 goals in a Stanley Cup game?

A. Eddie Gerard

B. Joe Malone

C. Frank McGee

D. Edouard Lalonde

3. To which team was the Stanley Cup first awarded?

A. Montréal Wanderers

B. Ottawa Silver Seven

C. Montréal Victorias

D. Montréal Amateur Athletic Association

1. B. Montréal

Although hockey had been played outdoors since the early 1800s, there were no set of rules and regulations that governed the game at the time. Born out of a collection of sports such as cricket and Irish Hurley, the early games of hockey would have been completely unrecognizable to the game played today. The earliest game in which two teams played under an agreed set of rules happened during a game in Montréal on March 3, 1875. The game was played on the campus of McGill University and was organized by Halifax native James Creighton. Having played the game most of his life on the frozen ponds near his home, Creighton sought to organize a game in Montréal with his new classmates. He got some of his old friends in Halifax to send a few dozen sticks to Montréal and booked the ice at the indoor Victoria Rink for the game. Although games like this had been played before, the difference this time was that Creighton set down a list of rules that organized the game into the first recognizable form of hockey. Because the game was played indoors on a limited ice surface, Creighton had to reduce the number of players to nine per side. The outdoor version of the game often involved as many as 20 players on each team. Two poles marked the goal area, and possibly for the first time, two players volunteered as goalkeepers, further supporting the idea that it was the first real game of hockey ever played. The game was won by Creighton's team, 2–1, and was said to have been a violent affair in which heads were bashed and female spectators fainted at the sight of such carnage.

2. C. Frank McGee

McGee was the first superstar in the game of hockey. The nephew of the famous Canadian politician Darcy McGee, Frank was a natural-born athlete, excelling in all sports, but hockey was his passion. Not long after taking up the sport, McGee quickly made a name for himself as the star of hockey's elite team, the Ottawa Silver Seven. McGee's most famous moment came in 1905, when his star-studded Ottawa club met a ragtag team from Dawson City, Yukon, in a battle for the right to be named the Champions of Lord Stanley's Cup. In the first game of the series, McGee was held to just one goal, though his team won the game 9–2. After that first game, all anyone could talk about was how the Dawson goaltender frustrated the great Frank McGee time and time again. This did not sit well with McGee. More determined than ever, he returned in game two with one purpose in mind. He scored four goals in the first half (games at the time were played in two 30-minute halves), and in the second half he exploded, scoring eight goals in under eight minutes, adding two in the dying minutes of the game for an incredible total of 14 goals in one game. No player has come close to beating or tying McGee's record, and no player ever will.

3. D. Montréal Amateur Athletic Association

At the end of the 1893 Amateur Hockey Association (AHA) season, the Cup was handed over to the league winners, the Montréal Amateur Athletic Association, without any other teams competing for the Cup in a playoff round. The first actual competition for the Stanley Cup happened one year later when three teams from the AHA vied for possession of the championship Cup. The Montréal AAAs won the Cup that year as well.

Questions 4 – 6

4. **What year did the Montréal Canadiens play their first game?**

   A. 1894

   B. 1901

   C. 1909

   D. 1910

5. **Which league formed the first fully professional league in hockey?**

   A. International Hockey League

   B. Eastern Canadian Hockey Association

   C. National Hockey Association

   D. Western Pennsylvania Hockey League

6. **Where was the first-ever artificial ice rink built?**

   A. London, England

   B. New York City, New York

   C. Vancouver, British Columbia

   D. Montréal, Québec

4. C. 1909

The Montréal Canadiens were born out of the division between the owners of the Eastern Canadian Hockey Association (ECHA) and a group of businessmen seeking their own franchise. Jimmy Gardner and J. Ambrose O'Brien joined forces and formed the National Hockey Association (NHA). Montréal had an already established group of teams, including the Montréal Amateur Athletic Association, the Montréal Wanderers, Montréal Shamrocks and the Montréal Victorias, but all were run and populated by English communities. French Montréal, long considered a second-class citizen, had no professional hockey team or arena to call their own. So when it was announced that the NHA would play its first game for the 1909 season, a new Montréal team took to the ice. Since the team was made up mostly of French Canadian players, naming the team proved rather easy. On December 4, 1909, at a meeting in room 129 of Montréal's Windsor Hotel, the Montréal Canadiens were born.

5. D. Western Pennsylvania Hockey League

For a long time it was believed that the International Hockey League, which formed in 1904, was the first-ever fully professional league in the history of the game. The league, which was based out of northern Michigan, had five teams and attracted a lot of the superstars of hockey. But another league out of the United States claims the prize as the first pro league. The Western Pennsylvania Hockey League (WPHL) started out as an amateur league in 1890 but made the switch to a fully pro league in 1902. Going professional meant the league was better organized, and the players were fully paid. The WPHL folded just two seasons later before eventually returning in 1907.

6. A. London, England

The first artificial ice surface was opened in Charing Cross in London, England, in 1876. The ice surface was designed and constructed by a professor named Gamgee. Gamgee built the 100-square-foot (9-square-metre) surface over a network of copper pipes that contained a mixture of glycerin and water, which circulated through the pipes after being chilled by ether. The freezing-cold pipes were then covered with water, and the artificial rink was born. Canada was slow to follow the example of the British, opening up its first artificial rink in 1911 in Vancouver and Victoria, British Columbia. Built by Lester and Frank Patrick, the artificial rink was a necessity in the temperate climate of BC, as natural ice rinks did not have a long life span in winter. One year later, Eastern Canada followed suit, and the first artificial rink opened in Toronto. By 1920 there were only four artificial rinks in the whole of Canada.

7. **Why did the Hamilton players strike during the 1925 NHL finals before they were set to play the Montréal Canadiens?**

A.   They thought the playoff format was unfair.

B.   They were afraid of playing the Canadiens.

C.   They were upset that the season was extended, and they did not receive proper pay.

D.   The league treated their head coach unfairly, and the team would not play until league president Frank Calder apologized.

8. **Name the only player to play both professional hockey and professional baseball in the major leagues.**

A.   Hobey Baker

B.   Jim Thorpe

C.   Eddie Gerrard

D.   Jim Riley

9. **Which Canadian city was home to a team known as the Swastikas?**

A.   St. John's, Newfoundland

B.   Kingston, Ontario

C.   Windsor, Nova Scotia

D.   Saint John, New Brunswick

7. C. They were upset that the season was extended, and they did not receive proper pay.

During a time when a team's starting player stayed in for almost an entire game, any extra games added to the schedule exacted a heavy toll on the player's physical condition. So when the NHL went from playing 24 games in 1923–24 to a 30-game schedule the following year, added two more franchises in Boston and in Montréal and expanded the playoff format to two rounds instead of one, players felt they should be paid accordingly. The players had a legitimate argument, because all the extra revenue from the new teams and the expanded playoffs was split evenly among the NHL owners, and the players got none. Other teams gave their players bonuses, but Hamilton did not, so the players refused to play against their NHL finals opponents, the Montréal Canadiens, until they were paid about $200 each. The league responded by threatening to fine each player $200 if they did not play in the NHL finals, but the Hamilton players decided they would rather quit the game than be taken advantage of. Montréal was declared the NHL champion and went on to face the Victoria Cougars in the Stanley Cup finals, which they lost three games to one. The Hamilton Tigers franchise was sold to a group in New York, and they became the New York Americans the following season.

8. D. Jim Riley

In the early days of professional hockey, many players did not make enough money to sustain themselves when the season ended. While many other hockey players got regular jobs to supplement their income, Jim Riley of the Pacific Coast Hockey Association's Seattle Metropolitans is the only athlete to ever play pro hockey and pro baseball (for the Boston Braves) during the 1910 major league season.

9. C. Windsor, Nova Scotia

Throughout the majority of human history, the Swastika was known by many cultures as a symbol for good luck, peace and good fortune. It wasn't until Adolf Hitler and his brutal Nazi regime that the Swastika became a symbol of extreme hatred and violence. So it seemed a perfectly normal symbol and name for the hockey team from Windsor, Nova Scotia, to use when they formed a new team in 1905. The Windsor Swastikas proudly displayed the symbol on their jerseys until 1916, and the team was known in the region as one of the top-notch clubs with an exciting brand of fast, high-scoring hockey.

10. **The first all-black hockey league was establised in what year?**

   A. 1894

   B. 1915

   C. 1927

   D. 1933

11. **When did the hockey net first "officially" appear?**

   A. 1860

   B. 1891

   C. 1897

   D. 1899

12. **Who is considered the inventor of the "modern" hockey net?**

   A. Paddy Moran

   B. Clint Benedict

   C. Percy LeSueur

   D. Hap Holmes

10. A. 1894

Years past, though no black player could even entertain the hope of getting a regular spot in the NHL or any other pro-league, black hockey players could find a place in the Maritimes Coloured Hockey League. Formed in 1894 in Nova Scotia, the league featured teams from across the Maritimes and lasted until 1930. The league was known for its fast action and high scoring. The games were played on an invitational basis and competition was more for fun than for glory. The focus on family fun met a need in the region and kept the seats full for over two decades.

11. D. 1899

Although it is possible that any enterprising hockey player might have thrown a net over the standard posts that marked the goal line, a report in a Halifax newspaper on January 6, 1899, officially mentions the use of a net in a game between two clubs from the Halifax region. Later that year, the Canadian Hockey League, before the start of the 1899–1900 season, adopted a similar design.

12. C. Percy LeSueur

Percy LeSueur was a student of the game. Not content to just play hockey, LeSueur was constantly looking to improve every aspect, from goaltender to coaching. Tired of the countless disputed goals scored in the upper part of the net, LeSueur added a crossbar to the frame, giving the net the same basic shape that is still seen today.

13. **When were goaltender pads first introduced?**

A. 1872

B. 1888

C. 1896

D. 1924

14. **Who is known as the father of hockey referees?**

A. Kerry Fraser

B. Fred Waghorne

C. Lord Thomas Haliburton

D. Frank Patrick

15. **Whom did the National Hockey Association board of governors want to exclude when they formed the National Hockey League (NHL) in 1917?**

A. Eddie Livingstone

B. J. Ambrose O'Brien

C. Leo Dandurand

D. John Molson

13. C.   1896 and D. 1924

Before the February 16, 1896, Stanley Cup match between the Montréal Victorias and the Winnipeg Victorias, Winnipeg goaltender George "Whitey" Merritt decided to change into some new equipment. The hundreds of fans gathered to watch the game were shocked to see Merritt put on a pair of cricket pads on the outside of his trousers to protect his legs. There are pictures of other goaltenders prior to Merritt wearing cricket pads, but Merritt gets credit for the invention for having worn them in a big game such as the Stanley Cup final.

The first modern goalie pads were created in 1924 by Emil Kenesky, when he modified a pair of cricket pads by stuffing and widening them to 12 inches (30 centimetres). The wider leather pads became popular with goaltenders, and another significant change in pad technology was not seen until Boston Bruins goaltender Rejean Lemelin wore the much lighter Aeroflex pads in the late 1980s.

14. B. Fred Waghorne

Fred Waghorne was one of the game's greatest innovators. At a time when the game had no official set of rules, Waghorne's quick on-ice decisions often became the governing laws of hockey that still exist today. Among his many contributions to the game, Waghorne was the first referee to use a whistle during a game and the first to use a faceoff, establishing a style and conviction that lasts to this day. In his career he refereed over 2400 hockey games, and he was elected into the Hockey Hall of Fame in the builder category in 1961. The builder category in the Hockey Hall of Fame celebrates those behind the scenes who have made a significant contribution and promoted the game of hockey for future generations.

15. A. Eddie Livingstone

Had Eddie Livingstone not been so good at his job, the NHL might have never come into existence. After buying his way into the old boys' club that was the National Hockey Association, Livingstone quickly made himself enemy number one among the other owners. During World War I, there was a shortage of quality players, and any sort of hockey talent was at a premium. Livingstone had a knack for signing good players and was irritatingly adept at exploiting loopholes in league regulations, making him unpopular with the older, established owners. At the end of the 1917 NHA season, the owners (all except Livingstone) got together at a Montréal hotel and decided to start a new league, effectively muscling out Livingstone's franchise. On November 26, 1917, it was announced that a new league had been formed, called the National Hockey League.

16. Which player died as a result of contracting the Spanish Influenza during the 1919 Stanley Cup finals?

A. Billy Coutu

B. Joe Hall

C. Newsy Lalonde

D. Georges Vezina

17. Who was the first NHL player to wear a helmet?

A. Howie Morenz

B. Dit Clapper

C. Eddie Gerard

D. George Owen

18. Name the first team to put player names on the back of their uniforms.

A. Toronto St. Pats

B. Boston Bruins

C. Philadelphia Quakers

D. New York Americans

16. B. Joe Hall

"Bad" Joe Hall was one of the toughest hockey players of his time, but he could not fight off the ravages of the Spanish Influenza that he contracted during the 1919 Stanley Cup finals. After spending several days in hospital, Hall succumbed to the deadly plague.

17. D. George Owen

Playing for the Boston Bruins in 1929, rookie defenceman George Owen briefly wore a leather football helmet. Despite the funny looks he got, Owen helped his team on their way to the Stanley Cup championship that year.

18. D. New York Americans

In order to make the game easier for an American audience not used to the game of hockey, the New York Americans was the first team to put player names on jerseys during the 1925–26 NHL season. The NHL did not make names on jerseys mandatory until 1978.

19. **Who is the only member of the New York Americans to finish number one in scoring?**

A. Lorne Carr

B. Dave "Sweeney" Schriner

C. Eddie Burke

D. Normie Himes

20. **Who was the all-time leader in scoring until Maurice Richard broke his record in 1952?**

A. Nels Stewart

B. Howie Morenz

C. Newsy Lalonde

D. Babe Dye

21. **With what team did the legendary King Clancy break into the NHL?**

A. Toronto St. Pats

B. Ottawa Senators

C. Québec Bulldogs

D. Montréal Canadiens

19. B. Dave "Sweeney" Schriner

A talented, speedy left winger, Dave "Swee-ney" Schriner led the league in scoring twice while playing for the terrible New York Americans. His entertaining style of hockey was more than welcome on a team struggling to bring fans into the stands. Another little known fact about Schriner was that he was the first Russian-born NHL star.

20. A. Nels Stewart

On November 8, 1952, Maurice Richard scored his 325th career goal to surpass the old king of scoring, Nels Stewart. Joining the Montréal Maroons for the 1925–26 season, Stewart shot straight to the top of the scoring championship and was a major factor in the Maroons' Stanley Cup victory, taking home the Hart trophy as the most valuable player in the league. He continued his consistent scoring throughout his career with the Maroons and the Boston Bruins, before finally finishing his career with the New York Americans. He was inducted to the Hockey Hall of Fame in 1962.

21. B. Ottawa Senators

Francis Michael "King" Clancy got his start with the Ottawa Senators for the 1921–22 NHL season. At 5 feet 7 inches, King Clancy was one of the smaller players out on the ice, but he made up for his lack of stature with his physical play and acid tongue. Clancy, describing his first pro camp, once said, "My first time out they tried to knock me around quite a bit. Every rookie has to go through this. Especially if the kid is only 5 foot 7 and weighed about as much as a sack of potatoes." Clancy won two Stanley Cups with the Senators before moving to the Toronto Maple Leafs in 1930–31.

22. How did goaltending legend Georges Vezina die?

A. Car accident

B. Spanish Influenza

C. Tuberculosis

D. Murdered by his wife

23. Which player led the NHL in scoring in 1918–19?

A. Frank Nighbor

B. Newsy Lalonde

C. Odie Cleghorn

D. Alf Skinner

22. C. Tuberculosis

After staring down the shots of some of the greatest players in the game, Georges Vezina died after a lengthy and painful battle with tuberculosis. On November 28, 1925, Vezina suited up to play in a game against the Pittsburgh Pirates, and though he had a fever, he still managed to stop every shot in the first period. But at the start of the second period, he could no longer fight off his illness and collapsed to the ice. Five months later, Vezina died from complications as a result of tuberculosis in his hometown of Chicoutimi, Québec.

23. B. Newsy Lalonde

Edouard "Newsy" Lalonde was the premiere scoring threat with the Montréal Canadiens in the early years of the NHL. During his entire career in the NHL, he was one of the biggest offensive threats on the ice at anytime, using his speed and great knowledge of how the game was played to get around obstacles.

24. In what year was the first women's hockey team formed?

A. 1889

B. 1891

C. 1909

D. 1922

25. What was the name of the NHL franchise in Hamilton?

A. Hamilton Tiger-Cats

B. Hamilton Steelers

C. Hamilton Roughnecks

D. Hamilton Tigers

24. B. 1891

It will always be disputed as to when the first game between all-women teams was actually played, but the first official recording of a game appeared in the *Ottawa Citizen* newspaper on February 11, 1891. Although the teams were not named, it was reported as an entertaining game in which the women played rather well. By 1894, regular women's games were popping up all around North America. In 1896, the *Ottawa Citizen* reported on one such women's game, saying, "Both teams played grandly and surprised hundreds of the sterner sex who went to the match expecting to see many ludicrous scenes and have many good laughs. Indeed, before they were there very long, their sympathies and admiration had gone out to the teams. The men became wildly enthusiastic."

25. D. Hamilton Tigers

The Hamilton Tigers were part of the NHL from 1920 to 1925. In their five years in the league, they never won the Stanley Cup and only made it into the playoffs once.

Chapter Two

Hockey's Greatest Quotations: Who Said What

---

26. "He shoots, he scores!"

A. Don Cherry

B. Danny Gallivan

C. Foster Hewitt

D. Bob Cole

27. "Sixty minutes of hell."

A. Maurice Richard

B. Jacques Plante

C. Tony Esposito

D. Glenn Hall

28. "There's no sense of loss. I held the record for a long time, and I hope to be around when he scores 3000 points."

A. Gordie Howe

B. Mark Messier

C. Maurice Richard

D. Wayne Gretzky

26. C. Foster Hewitt

The master broadcaster Foster Hewitt was the first person to use the much used and much imitated phrase, "He shoots, he scores!" At the tender age of 18, Hewitt uttered those legendary words during his inaugural broadcast on March 22, 1923, during a game at Toronto's Maple Leaf Gardens. Speaking to hockey historian Brian McFarlane, Hewitt admitted, "I didn't plan to use it. It just came out." And in time it seemed to catch the fancy of a lot of listeners.

27. D. Glenn Hall

Although he played in 551 consecutive games (including playoffs), won the Stanley Cup and boasted countless distinctions as one of the greatest goaltenders in the game, Glenn Hall always described his time on the ice as "Sixty minutes of hell." Hockey was his passion, but the intense pressures and the thousands of eyes watching his every move made his nervous system do strange things. Before most games he would throw up, and on the nights when he didn't toss his cookies, his team usually ended up losing. Said Hall about his weak nerves before a game, "I always felt I played better if I was physically ill before the game. If I wasn't sick, I felt I hadn't done everything I could to try to win." Now that's dedication to a cause! You can say what you will about his nerves, but just try standing in the way of a Bobby Hull slapshot with no mask and see what things you toss up before a game.

28. A. Gordie Howe

It was a long-held belief that Gordie Howe's total career points records would never be broken, but then a young man by the name of Wayne Gretzky came along, and all seemed possible. Able to rack up over 200 points in four separate seasons, it was just a matter of time before Gretzky caught up to his boyhood hero Gordie Howe. On the night of October 15, 1989, Gretzky's Los Angeles Kings rolled into the city that once was lucky enough to call him their own, to play the Edmonton Oilers. Gretzky had tied Howe's total point mark of 1850 a few days earlier, and all eyes were on Gretzky to break Howe's record, including Mr. Hockey himself. Everyone held their collective breath throughout the game as the first, second and early third period went by without Gretzky registering a point. The record-breaking point finally came late in the game when Gretzky shovelled a backhand in past Oilers goaltender Bill Ranford for his 1851 point in just his 780th game. Howe's feat had taken him 26 years and 1767 games. After the goal went in, the game was stopped, and Howe came out of the stands and personally congratulated Gretzky.

Questions 29 – 31

29. **"I'm crazy, but not that crazy!"**

   A.   Jacques Plante

   B.   Patrick Roy

   C.   Ron Hextall

   D.   Gerry Cheevers

30. **The stress of having to score a goal every night is one thing, but the stress of going into a game knowing you're going to have to fight is something totally different."**

   A.   Tie Domi

   B.   Chris Nilan

   C.   Rob Ray

   D.   John Kordic

31. **"All hockey players are bilingual. They know English and profanity."**

   A.   Gordie Howe

   B.   Pat Lafontaine

   C.   Mark Messier

   D.   Jacques Lemaire

29. D. Gerry Cheevers

It is common knowledge among those who have ever suited up for a high-level game of hockey that goaltenders have to be a little crazy to stand in the way of speeding, frozen rubber pucks. But goaltenders have their limits. Gerry Cheevers' moment came one day when his Boston Bruins met up against the Chicago Blackhawks and their sniper Bobby Hull. Bobby Hull was known to have the hardest slapshot in the league, clocked in at over 100 kilometres per hour. As if he didn't give goaltenders enough problems with the hard shot, Hull had a penchant for whizzing pucks close to the heads of players he didn't like.

30. C. Rob Ray

Rob Ray was never a high-scoring player, and he used his fists to make his way into the NHL. But all those fights can wear on the emotions of a player, as described by Ray in his quotation.

31. A. Gordie Howe

Although Gordie Howe portrayed himself off the ice as one of the great gentlemen of the game, his on-ice conduct was one of the most vicious. Being one of the toughest players on the ice, he was often on the receiving end of a litany of verbal abuse.

Questions 32 – 34

32. **"Hockey captures the essence of Canadian experience in the New World. In a land so inescapably and inhospitably cold, hockey is the chance of life, and an affirmation that despite the deathly chill of winter we are alive."**

    A.   Hugh Maclennan

    B.   Leonard Cohen

    C.   Stephen Leacock

    D.   Farley Mowatt

33. **"How would you like a job where, every time you make a mistake, a big red light goes on and 18,000 people boo?"**

    A.   Patrick Roy

    B.   Ed Belfour

    C.   Jacques Plante

    D.   Glenn Hall

34. **"Some people skate to the puck. I skate to where the puck is going to be."**

    A.   Sidney Crosby

    B.   Guy Lafleur

    C.   Maurice Richard

    D.   Wayne Gretzky

32. C. Stephen Leacock

Famed Canadian author and humorist Stephen Leacock best summarized Canadians' affection for the game of hockey as our continuing battle against the cold country we all have decided to inhabit. With today's technology, it is now possible to play hockey in the middle of a desert, but you don't see Saudi Arabia with a national hockey team.

33. C. Jacques Plante

Jacques Plante was not your average goaltender. He liked to knit before games and was always getting under the skin of Montréal Canadiens head coach Toe Blake with his eccentric behaviour. So it's no surprise to learn of Plante's response when asked a multitude of questions by reporters after one particularly bad game.

34. D. Wayne Gretzky

This quote may be attributed to Wayne Gretzky, but he gives credit for the idea to his father, Walter. When Wayne was a kid, his dad always taught him to skate to where the puck was going to end up, because that's where it would be open. Watch any of Gretzky's old tapes from his playing days and you will see the theory put into practice to perfection.

35. "This record honours all French Canadians."

A.   Jean Beliveau

B.   Patrick Roy

C.   Maurice Richard

D.   Newsy Lalonde

36. "Do you believe in miracles?"

A.   Herb Brooks

B.   Al Michaels

C.   Phil Esposito

D.   Tony Esposito

37. "I can't believe you're coming to me with this the day after we won the Cup."

A.   Maurice Richard

B.   Bryan Trottier

C.   Patrick Roy

D.   Wayne Gretzky

35. C. Maurice Richard

To try to put into a few lines what Maurice Richard meant to French Canadians in the 1950s is a difficult task. The idea of French nationalism was just beginning to take hold in Québec, and Richard was looked upon as a hero of the entire province. He was everyone's favourite player and proudly represented the place and culture from which he came. When he scored his 45th goal during the 1944–45 season, Richard broke Joe Malone's single-season goal record, something many thought to be unattainable. After the game, quote-hungry reporters swarmed around Richard looking for a juicy quotation for their papers. Well aware of the support he received from the Montréal Canadiens fans and the people of Québec, Richard said, "This record honours all French Canadians." From that point on he became a legend in the province.

36. B. Al Michaels

In late '70s and into the '80s, the Soviets were considered the best hockey players in the world. They were pegged as the ones who were going to walk away with the gold medal in the 1980 Winter Olympics, without breaking a sweat. The United States was not expected to go anywhere in the medal rounds with a team made up of amateur players, but they managed, to everyone's surprise, to make it into the semifinals against the Soviet squad. The problem was that no one thought the Americans would even come close to winning the game against the far superior Soviets. But under the guidance of head coach Herb Brooks, the ragtag bunch of American hockey players pulled off the upset of the decade, beating the Russians in the semifinal by a close score of 4–3. At the end of the game, ABC sportscaster Al Michaels uttered these famous words, which still resonate in hockey today.

37. D. Wayne Gretzky

Wayne Gretzky and Peter Pocklington were never the greatest of friends while the "Great One" was playing for the Oilers. Pocklington was a businessman first, and often-times his decisions made him an unlikable person. Just days after Gretzky led the Oilers to yet another Stanley Cup in 1988, Pocklington approached Gretzky with a potential trade offer from Vancouver, to which Gretzky replied with this quote. Just five days after his wedding, Gretzky got a call from the Los Angeles Kings, and he knew then that his days in Edmonton were over.

38. "We get nose jobs all the time in the NHL, and we don't even have to go to the hospital."

A.   Don Cherry

B.   Chris Nilan

C.   Brad Park

D.   Dave Schultz

39. "My pre-game meal on the road is a steak and a blonde."

A.   Derek Sanderson

B.   Jeremy Roenick

C.   Ray Emery

D.   John Kordic

40. "I was talking to my goalposts."

A.   Billy Smith

B.   Ray Emery

C.   Patrick Roy

D.   Bernie Parent

38. C. Brad Park

During those years when most players elected not to wear helmets in the rough and tumble world of professional hockey, it was a natural occurrence for some players to have their noses rearranged on a regular basis. Brad Park had a few "hockey style" surgeries of his own.

39. A. Derek Sanderson

Derek Sanderson was a well-known and out-spoken disturber of the peace. On the ice he was one of the most annoying players to play against, and off the ice, he equally stirred certain sentiments among the public. On occasion, the one-time 1968 rookie of the year lived up to his reputation a little too much with wonderful quotations such as this one.

40. C. Patrick Roy

One of Patrick Roy's most famous and lasting images of his great career was the chats he had with his goalposts before each game of the 1986 Stanley Cup playoffs. Curious New York reporters gathered around the rookie goaltender after one game of the 1986 Conference Finals and asked him just what he was doing at the end of the national anthems when he stuck his head inside the net. Roy simply responded, "I was talking to my goalposts."

Questions 41 – 43

41. **"You don't have to be crazy to be a goalie, but it helps."**

   A.   Jacques Plante
   B.   Bernie Parent
   C.   Grant Fuhr
   D.   Martin Brodeur

42. **"If I had played the full three periods of that game, we would have won."**

   A.   Patrick Roy
   B.   Olaf Kolzig
   C.   Dominik Hasek
   D.   Vladislav Tretiak

43. **Who said this of Montréal Canadiens legend Maurice Richard? "When he was coming down on you, the puck glued to the end of his stick, his eyes were flashing and gleaming like lights of a pinball machine. It was frightening."**

   A.   Frank Brimsek
   B.   Turk Broda
   C.   Glenn Hall
   D.   Terry Sawchuk

41. B. Bernie Parent

Although he never said much in English, when Bernie Parent did choose to speak in his second language, he always got his point across. The eccentric goaltender began his NHL career with the Boston Bruins but is better known for his time between the pipes for the Philadelphia Flyers. He won two Stanley Cups with the Flyers in 1974 and 1975.

42. D. Vladislav Tretiak

Known as one of the premiere netminders on the international stage, Tretiak played in some of the most memorable games in hockey history. Although Canada won the Summit Series in 1972, Tretiak was the only reason the Soviet team was able to take the series into the final game. He was a reliable goaltender and had a passion to see everything through to the end. But the moment he regrets most in his career was when he was taken out of goal during the 1980 Winter Olympics semifinal game against the United States. After a fluke goal by U.S. forward Mark Johnson, Tretiak was pulled in favour of backup goaltender Vladimir Myshkin. The United States went on to upset the Soviet team and eventually won the gold medal. Years later, Tretiak still believes he would have made the difference in that game for the Soviets but, as he said, "It wasn't my idea. The coach decided. In that situation, you don't ask; you don't argue." Four years later, Tretiak was in goal to help the Soviets win the gold medal at the 1984 Winter Olympics in Sarajevo.

43. C. Glenn Hall

On October 19, 1957, Maurice Richard scored his 500th career goal against the Chicago Blackhawks goaltender Glenn Hall. Unfortunately, that was not the only goal scored by Richard against Hall, who had to contend with the Canadiens captain's remarkable ability to put the puck into the net. When Richard announced his retirement from the game, it prompted goaltenders such as Hall to admit they were not sad to see those intense eyes staring them down anymore.

Questions 44 – 45

44. **"If a little guy like me is to succeed in the big leagues, I have to show all those guys, big or small, that I'll stand up for my rights. I don't care if it's Jeff Beukeboom or Mario Lemieux that I hit."**

   A.   Theoren Fleury

   B.   Tie Domi

   C.   Martin St. Louis

   D.   Darius Kasparaitis

45. **Which player prompted the great Bobby Orr to say, "What he could do, I couldn't do. He could do more things than any other player I've ever seen."**

   A.   Wayne Gretzky

   B.   Pavel Bure

   C.   Teemu Selanne

   D.   Mario Lemieux

44. A. Theoren Fleury

At 5 foot 6 and weighing only 160 pounds, Theoren Fleury was always the smallest guy on the ice, but he more than made up for his deficiency in size by playing an intense, passionate style of hockey. It also helped that he could score just like his larger counterparts. His best season came during the 1990–91 NHL season with the Calgary Flames, when he scored 51 goals and 53 assists. The only problem was the constant scrutiny placed on his game because of his size. Fleury had to always up his game, and after several years of playing at such an aggressive level, his career and personal life began to unravel. After several well-publicized battles with illegal substances, Fleury ended his NHL career with the Chicago Blackhawks in 2002–03.

45. D. Mario Lemieux

Very few players could elicit such praise from one of the greatest players in the game. From his first moments in the professional ranks, Mario Lemieux established himself as one of the rare, true talents in hockey. His amazing moves, accurate shot and leadership abilities made him one of the best players in hockey, and had he not had all those back problems and his bout with cancer, he might have been considered THE greatest.

46. Fill in the blanks with the first name from one of the players listed below:
" _____ loved to play hockey more than anyone loved anything, and when he realized that he would never play again..._____ died of a broken heart."

A. Joe Hall

B. Georges Vezina

C. Charlie Gardiner

D. Howie Morenz

47. "That year will always stand out because we were older players. There was a definite feeling that some of us wouldn't get another chance."

A. Glenn Hall

B. Bob Gainey

C. Ray Bourque

D. Johnny Bower

46. D. Howie Morenz

After such a brilliant career, Howie Morenz's life ended with tragedy. After two years away from the Canadiens organization, with the Chicago Blackhawks and then with the New York Rangers, Morenz returned to the Montréal Canadiens for the start of the 1936–37 regular season. He was happy to be back in Montréal and was going through a career revival when tragedy struck on January 28, 1937. That night, the Canadiens took on the Chicago Blackhawks at the Montréal Forum under the watchful eye of a capacity crowd. The mood was upbeat in the Forum as the Canadiens battled for the top of their division, and Morenz was in peak form. But the mood quickly changed on one play in particular, when Morenz raced into the corner to pick up the puck. His skate got caught in between the ice and the boards just as big Chicago defenceman Earl Siebert came racing in from behind and crashed into him. Morenz's body twisted from the collision, but his leg stayed in the same spot. People at the Forum that night swore they could hear Morenz's leg break from the impact.

At the hospital, doctors told Morenz it was unlikely that he would ever play hockey again as a result of his injuries. Although he had a constant stream of visitors to his hospital bed, Morenz sank deeper and deeper into depression with each passing day spent away from his team. After lying in bed for a month, a tired and frustrated Morenz decided he'd had enough hospital rest and was going to leave the hospital, no matter what risks. On March 8, 1937, still wearing the plaster cast on his leg, Morenz forced himself out of bed, took one step and fell to the floor, dying on the spot. Doctors reported the cause of death as a "cardiac deficiency and acute excitement," but his friends knew that his death was partially caused by the pain of knowing that he could never return to the game he loved. Teammate Aurel Joliat best summed up what happened to Howie Morenz in this quote.

47. D. Johnny Bower

Bower was prompted to say this because the last time the Toronto Maple Leafs won the Stanley Cup in 1967, the majority of the team was composed of veteran players near the end of their careers. When the playoffs started in 1967, no one expected the Leafs to go very far. Sportswriters made jokes about the players' age, saying that they belonged in an old folks home rather than in the Stanley Cup playoffs. But instead of discouraging the team, all the criticism about their age united the team. Veterans Red Kelly, Terry Sawchuk, and the oldest of them all, Johnny Bower, were the core of the Stanley Cup–winning team that beat the Chicago Blackhawks in the semifinals and surprised a strong Montréal team by winning the finals in six games. The "Over-the-Hill-Gang," as they were called, overcame all odds and spoiled the Canadiens' plans, but the veteran movement in Toronto only lasted that one season. As veteran Allan Stanley best put it, "When they let me go for a youth movement in 1968, I often joked, 'They'll never win another Cup without me.' But geez, I didn't mean it."

48. "To the people across Canada, we're try-
ing our best. For the people that booed
us, geez, I'm really...all of the guys are
really disheartened and we're disillu-
sioned and disappointed in some of the
people."

A.   Paul Henderson

B.   Phil Esposito

C.   Wayne Gretzky

D.   Ken Dryden

49. "I was going to number 66 whether he
wanted it or not."

A.   Larry Murphy

B.   Dale Hawerchuk

C.   Wayne Gretzky

D.   Ray Bourque

50. "We know we're going to go in and win
game six and bring it back for game
seven."

A.   Dominik Hasek

B.   Brian Propp

C.   Patrick Roy

D.   Mark Messier

48. B. Phil Esposito

When the Canadian team suffered their first two losses to the Soviets during the Summit Series in 1972, they began to feel the weight of fan and media pressure. When the series moved to the Pacific Coliseum in Vancouver, the Canadian crowd turned on their team for their perceived lack of effort against the Soviets, and following several periods of vicious booing, Phil Esposito finally had had enough of the crowd. After the game, which the Canadians lost 5–3, Esposito skated over to the nearest microphone and vented his anger and disappointment to the Canadian crowd. But things began to turn around for Team Canada and they eventually went on to win the series.

49. C. Wayne Gretzky

The 1987 fight for the Canada Cup was billed as a replay of the series that had defined Canadian hockey 15 years earlier when Team Canada found itself once again battling for the title of hockey supremacy against the mighty Soviet Union. The three-game series started with the Soviets winning at the Montréal Forum in overtime. Canada answered with an overtime win of its own in the second game, thanks to a beautiful goal by Mario Lemieux. In the final game, the Soviets pulled ahead 3–0 in the first period, but Team Canada roared back to tie the game. Tied five apiece in the late stages of the game, Canada finally got its big chance. Dale Hawerchuk got the puck to Gretzky who, with Larry Murphy and Mario Lemieux, streaked in on the Soviet zone. Gretzky fed Lemieux a perfect pass, and Lemieux slapped the puck into the top corner of the net for the game and series winning goal. Canada was once again at the top of the world. After the game, Gretzky commented to reporters that passing to Mario was his only option.

50. D. Mark Messier

After 54 years without the Stanley Cup, the New York Ranger faithful began to believe all the talk of a curse. The curse looked more and more like a reality for the Rangers in the 1994 Conference Finals when they met the New Jersey Devils and fell behind in the series three games to two. But the Rangers captain Mark Messier was determined to win the series and move into the finals against the Vancouver Canucks. However, everywhere the Rangers went, they were constantly reminded of the curse against them. Despite this, Messier continued to believe in his teammates, prompting him to make a speech to them before game six in which he predicted a victory. True to his words, Messier scored a hat trick to lead the Rangers to a game six victory and eventually to a Stanley Cup championship.

Chapter Three

Crazy Hockey Nicknames

51. What player was known for being "One-Eyed"?

A. Frank McGee

B. Red Kelly

C. Clint Benedict

D. Nels Stewart

52. Who would have been good enough to be called "The China Wall"?

A. Johnny Bower

B. Ken Dryden

C. Glenn Hall

D. Charlie Hodge

53. What poor soul's last name was attached to this unfortunate nickname, "In-the-wrong-place-at-the-wrong-time-_____"?

A. Dave Reece

B. Wayne Thomas

C. Nick Ricci

D. Gary Smith

51. A. Frank McGee

The legend of McGee only continues to grow with each passing year. Said to be one of the greatest hockey players to have ever lived, McGee's legend takes on a greater dimension when you consider that he played most of his career with only one good eye. Early in his career, McGee's Ottawa club met up against the tough Montréal Wanderers, a team with a reputation for their overly aggressive physical play. One of the toughest players on the team was Pokey Leahy, and that night he was gunning for Ottawa's star player. Early in the game, Leahy caught McGee with a vicious check that sent McGee crashing to the ice with a steady stream of blood gushing from a wound on his head. As a result of the injury, McGee permanently lost the vision in his left eye. Most people at the time thought he would retire from the game because the fast-paced action would have been difficult for a man with limited depth perception, but McGee defied all odds and returned to the game as soon as the doctors gave him the green light. "One-Eyed" McGee was not really affected by his vision loss and continued to dominate until his retirement.

52. A. Johnny Bower

Johnny "China Wall" Bower was the goaltender who saw the Toronto Maple Leafs through their dynasty during the 1960s. Bower's age and amazing ability are the two key ingredients in explaining his nickname. Being compared to the ancient Great Wall of China, Bower was always teased by his teammates that he had never been a young man. Couple this with his ability to repel pucks, and "China Wall" seemed to be a fitting nickname for the Maple Leaf goaltender.

53. A. Dave Reece

If Dave Reece had his choice, "In-the-wrong-place-at-the-wrong-time-Reece" was not a nickname he would wish to be remembered by, but after one particularly bad game, hockey history knows him by no other moniker. Following Reece's successful career in the minors, the Boston Bruins finally called him up for the 1975–76 regular season. After several mediocre games under his belt, Reece was put in nets for an insignificant game on February 7, 1976, against the Toronto Maple Leafs. It just so happened that it was the same night when the Leafs Darryl Sittler scored his record six goals and four assists—all on the unlucky Reece. The newspapers were rather unkind the next day and dubbed the poor goaltender "In-the-wrong-place-at-the-wrong-time-Reece." Said Reece after the game, "It was beach ball city. It just wasn't my night, and Darryl was pure magic. The Leafs were going nuts, but I never realized he was doing all the scoring or going for a record. That's the fun of sports, but sometimes I wonder why I wasn't pulled after five or six goals."

54. Which player was fast enough to be called "The Rocket"?

A. Howie Morenz

B. Maurice Richard

C. Ted Kennedy

D. Alex Delvecchio

55. Which player was known as "The Pocket Rocket"?

A. Dickie Moore

B. Ted Lindsay

C. Bill Hay

D. Henri Richard

56. Who was good enough to be called "The Great One"?

A. Sidney Crosby

B. Eric Lindros

C. Wayne Gretzky

D. Mario Lemieux

54. B. Maurice Richard

Maurice Richard did not start out as "The Rocket." The nickname came about after one reporter got a look at the speedy young rookie during training camp and wrote about the Rocket in the paper the next day. From then on he became known as Maurice "The Rocket" Richard.

55. D. Henri Richard

Like his older brother, Henri Richard developed his game around his blistering speed, and since his older brother had already taken "The Rocket" as a famous moniker, Henri was given the lesser though still powerful nickname of "The Pocket Rocket."

56. C. Wayne Gretzky

Not the most difficult of questions, but Wayne Gretzky is and will always be known as the "The Great One." With a career such as his—establishing 61 held and shared records, four Stanley Cups, countless awards and being a true gentleman of the game—it is likely that over time, he will be known as "The Greatest One."

57. What mediocre goaltender was called "Pokey"?

A.   Eddie Mio

B.   Eldon Reddick

C.   Roberto Romano

D.   Kari Takko

58. Which old time hockey player was dubbed the "Phantom"?

A.   Eddie Gerrard

B.   Joe Malone

C.   Jim Riley

D.   Lester Patrick

59. Which NHL enforcer earned the nickname "The Tiger"?

A.   Tie Domi

B.   Chris Nilan

C.   Sprague Leghorn

D.   Dave Williams

57. B. Eldon Reddick

Eldon "Pokey" Reddick was never a star in the NHL. He was known more for his unique name than his goaltending, but the journeyman goaltender served his teams in whatever city he found himself. "Pokey" was the goaltender for the Winnipeg Jets from 1986 to 1989, before jumping to the Edmonton Oilers and ending his brief career with the Florida Panthers in 1994.

58. B. Joe Malone

The "Phantom" Joe Malone was one of the original superstars of the game. Playing most of his career with the old Québec Bulldogs and the Montréal Canadiens, Malone earned the nickname because of his unique skating ability, which made him appear to move swiftly between opponents like a phantom. During the first season of the NHL with the Montréal Canadiens, the Phantom scored 44 goals in just 20 games.

59. D. Dave Williams

With 3966 career penalty minutes, Dave "The Tiger" Williams was no saint when it came to his on-ice play. He earned the nickname by attacking his opponents with the ferocity of a tiger. Williams summed up his philosophical approach to the game: "If you want to find out how great of an all-round player you are, go stand toe-to-toe with some guy 6 feet 3, 230 pounds and then go play the next shift. Not many guys can do that."

CRAZY HOCKEY NICKNAMES73

Questions 60 – 62

60. Who is known as the "Finnish Flash"?

A. Saku Koivu

B. Jari Kurri

C. Teemu Selanne

D. Ilkka Sinisalo

61. Who was known as the "Chicoutimi Cucumber"?

A. Didier Pitre

B. Georges Vezina

C. Jean Beliveau

D. Aurel Joliat

62. Who is known simply as "The Dominator"?

A. Ron Hextall

B. Dominik Hasek

C. Curtis Joseph

D. Patrick Roy

60. C. Teemu Selanne

After scoring 76 goals in his rookie season, Teemu Selanne earned himself the nickname the "Finnish Flash" for his amazing speed and his flare for the dramatic. No goalie could predict what the Finnish Flash would do on the ice, and once he scored, his celebrations were just as flashy as his goals.

61. B. Georges Vezina

Georges Vezina backstopped the Montréal Canadiens from 1910 to 1926. During his reign as the Canadiens goaltender, Vezina set the standard for all goaltenders to follow with his lightning-fast reflexes and excellent puck-handling skills. But it was his extremely calm demeanour in the face of speeding hockey pucks and 90-kilogram players crashing the net that earned him the nickname the "Chicoutimi Cucumber," being that he was from Chicoutimi and was cool as a cucumber.

62. B. Dominik Hasek

Dominik Hasek's skills were so prolific during his best years in the 1990s that he earned the nickname the "Dominator," for his ability to completely dominate a game by his mere presence on the ice. From 1993 to 2001, he won six Vezina Trophies and two Hart Trophies as the most valuable player in the league.

63. Which tough guy is known as "The Hammer"?

A.   Marty McSorley

B.   Rob Ray

C.   Tim Hunter

D.   Dave Schultz

64. Who was known as the "Babe Ruth of Hockey"?

A.   Bill Cook

B.   Nels Stewart

C.   Howie Morenz

D.   Cooney Weiland

65. What was one of the colourful names given to goaltender Clint Benedict?

A.   "Praying Benny"

B.   "Scarface"

C.   Clint "Pretty Boy" Benedict

D.   "Toothless Benny"

63. D. Dave Schultz

As an integral member of the Philadelphia Flyers' "Broad Street Bullies," Dave "The Hammer" Schultz had quite the reputation around the league for his habit of dropping his gloves and fighting anyone who got in his way. Although his penalty minutes did not match those of other fighting greats such as Tiger Williams and Tie Domi, Schultz was well known as one of the toughest fighters to play the game, hence his nickname.

64. C. Howie Morenz

Between 1923 and 1933, Howie Morenz was the greatest player in the NHL. He led the Montréal Canadiens to three Stanley Cups, won three Hart Trophies as the NHL's most valuable player and took home two Art Ross Trophies as the top scorer. During a time when hockey was struggling through the Depression for a stable fan base, especially in the United States, whenever Morenz rolled into town, fans would show up in droves just to see him play hockey. His blistering speed and ability to score goals when the team needed it the most prompted many comparisons to Babe Ruth of New York Yankee fame.

65. A. "Praying Benny"

"Praying Benny" and "Tumbling Clint" were nicknames for Clint Benedict that referenced his predilection for falling to the ice to make a save during a time in hockey when goaltenders were given a two-minute penalty for falling to the ice. Benedict became so adept at feigning a fall to the ice that referees around the league had trouble figuring out whether he actually fell to the ice on purpose or not. After frustrating the referees in his pre-NHL days, when Benedict entered the NHL in 1917, referees brought their complaints to President Frank Calder. Tired of all the complaints from referees and goaltenders, Calder acquiesced and changed the rules, allowing goaltenders to fall to the ice to make a save.

Questions 66 – 69

66. What was Howie Morenz commonly referred to as?

A. The "Speeding Bullet"

B. The "Stratford Streak"

C. The "Montréal Master"

D. The "Golden Boy"

67. Whose accurate shot and blistering slapper earned him the nickname "Old Poison"?

A. Nels Stewart

B. Elmer Lach

C. Stan Mikita

D. Doug Gilmour

68. Which goal scorer was known as "Boom Boom"?

A. Bobby Hull

B. Bernie Geoffrion

C. Ted Kennedy

D. Stan Mikita

69. Who was known as "Mr. Zero"?

A. Clint Benedict

B. Georges Hainsworth

C. Frank Brimsek

D. Terry Sawchuk

66. B. The "Stratford Streak"

Among his many other nicknames, Howie Morenz was most commonly known as the "Stratford Streak." A native of the Stratford, Ontario area, Morenz played his pre-professional days for one of the local clubs and earned himself the nickname because of the way he could blast by his other opponents, appearing as a streak of light in their eyes.

67. A. Nels Stewart

Nels Stewart once held the record for the most career goals in the NHL before Maurice Richard smashed that record. In Stewart's illustrious career, he scored 324 goals, winning the Stanley Cup with the Montréal Maroons in his rookie year. His shot was so accurate that it was said to be poisonous, because it could kill the hopes of his opponents, hence his nickname "Old Poison."

68. B. Bernie Geoffrion

Long before Bobby Hull had players jumping out of the way of his blistering slapshots, the Montréal Canadiens Bernie "Boom Boom" Geoffrion had the most powerful shot in the league. His incredible shot helped him to the scoring title in 1955 and made him the second player in NHL history to break the 50-goal mark. Geoffrion used the slapshot during a time in the league when most players were wristing or snapping the puck. Geoffrion started it, but Bobby Hull perfected it.

69. C. Frank Brimsek

When Frank Brimsek first joined the NHL in the 1938–39 season with the Boston Bruins, he made an immediate impression on the league. When the Boston Bruins number one goaltender Cecil "Tiny" Thompson suffered a severe injury, the Bruins called up a young kid from the Providence Reds of the American Hockey League to play out the rest of the season. Brimsek did more than just fill in for Thompson; he took over his job. Brimsek had an incredible first season with a goals-against-average of 1.56 and an amazing 10 shutouts. All those shutouts earned him the apt nickname "Mr. Zero."

Questions 70 – 72

70. Which legendary goaltender was known as "Ukey"?

A. Terry Sawchuk

B. Lorne Worsley

C. Walter Broda

D. Jim Henry

71. Who was known as "The Grate One"?

A. Pat Lafontaine

B. Steve Yzerman

C. Jari Kurri

D. Esa Tikkanen

72. Which famous line was known as the "Punch Line"?

A. Woody Dumart, Milt Schidmt, Bobby Bauer

B. Gordie Howe, Sid Abel, Ted Lindsay

C. Elmer Lach, Maurice Richard, Toe Blake

D. Wayne Gretzky, Jari Kurri, Dave Semenko

70. A. Terry Sawchuk

Terry Sawchuk was not called "Ukey" because of some special love of the ukulele, but simply because of his Ukrainian heritage.

71. D. Esa Tikkanen

Gretzky's teammate during the 1980s, Esa Tikkanen had a unique talent for annoying or grating on the nerves of his opponents with his relentless fore checking and constant trash talking.

72. C. Elmer Lach, Maurice Richard, Toe Blake

Starting during the 1944–45 NHL season, the line of Elmer Lach, Maurice Richard and Toe Blake was the premiere line in the league. That season, Maurice Richard scored 50 goals in 50 games, Elmer Lach won the scoring title recording a league record 54 assists, and Toe Blake rounded out the top three in scoring. The line not only could score but were also well known for their hitting abilities. They remained the "Punch Line" until injuries and retirement forced the Canadiens coach to put other players with Richard.

73. Who was known as the "Golden Jet"?

A. Brett Hull

B. Dickie Moore

C. Bobby Hull

D. Mike Bossy

74. Who is known simply as "Mr. Hockey"?

A. Don Cherry

B. Gordie Howe

C. Bobby Orr

D. Phil Esposito

75. Name the team that had one of the most dominant forward lines in the 1970s known as the "French Connection."

A. Montréal Canadiens

B. St. Louis Blues

C. Buffalo Sabres

D. New York Rangers

Answers 73 – 75

73. C. Bobby Hull

Hockey's golden boy got the nickname "Golden Jet" because of his golden locks and speed. He was young, handsome and strong—the perfect image for the NHL. His looks helped sell hockey, but his skills kept him in the game—fast skating, a deadly slapshot and scoring that put the Chicago Blackhawks in the 1961 Stanley Cup final.

74. B. Gordie Howe

Nicknamed "Mr. Hockey," Howe played professional hockey over six decades, amassed some of the most incredible statistics in the game, became an ambassador for hockey and a role model for kids. There were better skaters and better scorers, but no one matched Howe's intensity and consistency. Even in his 50s, Howe played all 80 games during the season and recorded 15 goals and 26 assists with the Hartford Whalers in 1979–80.

75. C. Buffalo Sabres

Gilbert Perreault, Richard Martin and Rene Robert, one of the most offensive trios of the time, helping the expansion Buffalo Sabres into the Stanley Cup finals by 1975. Richard Martin broke the 50-goal mark two years in a row, and Perreault and Robert both broke the 100-point mark on several occasions. Eventually Robert was traded to the Colorado Rockies in 1979, and Martin suffered a career-ending knee injury in 1980.

Chapter Four

The World of the Goaltender

76. Who was the last goaltender selected first overall in the NHL Entry Draft?

A.   Patrick Roy

B.   Cam Ward

C.   Rick Dipietro

D.   Marc-Andre Fleury

77. Who was the first goaltender to be selected first overall in the NHL Entry Draft?

A.   Ed Belfour

B.   Ken Dryden

C.   Michel Plasse

D.   Rick Dipietro

78. Who is the only goaltender to win consecutive Hart Trophies?

A.   Jacques Plante

B.   Glenn Hall

C.   Ken Dryden

D.   Dominik Hasek

76. D. Marc-Andre Fleury

After a brilliant career in junior hockey, the Pittsburgh Penguins made the easy choice of selecting Marc-Andre Fleury as their number one pick in the 2003 NHL Entry Draft. The Pittsburgh Penguins had suffered through several years without a quality goaltender, and they swapped their third-round selection with the Florida Panthers just to get Fleury.

77. C. Michel Plasse

Michel Plasse was selected number one overall in the 1968 NHL Amateur Entry Draft by the Montréal Canadiens. Although the Canadiens originally drafted Plasse, he got his start in the NHL with the St. Louis Blues, before jumping back to the Canadiens, then the Kansas City Scouts, the Pittsburgh Penguins and the Colorado Rockies. He ended his career in 1982 with the Québec Nordiques.

78. D. Dominik Hasek

With goals-against-averages of 2.27 in 1997 and 2.09 in 1998, it's easy to see why Dominik Hasek was voted the most valuable player in the NHL two years in a row. During those two years, Hasek helped the Buffalo Sabres become one of the premiere clubs in the league.

79. Who was the first goaltender to wear a mask?

A.   Jacques Plante

B.   Clint Benedict

C.   George Hainsworth

D.   Elizabeth Graham

80. Who holds the dubious distinction of recording the most losses suffered by a NHL goaltender in a single season?

A.   Gary Smith

B.   Doug Favell

C.   Denis Heron

D.   Peter Sidorkiewicz

81. Name the only goaltender to lose a game without ever having given up a goal.

A.   Vincent Riendeau

B.   Kelly Hrudey

C.   Mario Gosselin

D.   Brian Hayward

79. D. Elizabeth Graham

Although Clint Benedict was the first NHL player to wear a mask in the net, he wasn't the first hockey player to seek protection from flying frozen pucks. That distinction goes to Elizabeth Graham, who protected the net for the Queen's University women's hockey team during the 1927 season; she wore a fencing mask to protect herself from injury. Guarding the nets for Queen's Golden Gaels, Graham wanted some protection from flying sticks and deflected pucks so she grabbed a fencing mask from the Queen's fencing locker room, establishing one of hockey's most recognizable fashion statements.

80. A. Gary Smith

We have to feel sorry for the California Golden Seals 1970–71 goaltender Gary Smith. It wasn't that he was a bad goaltender; Smith just had one of the worst teams in the league that decade in front of him. Playing in 71 of the team's 78 league games, Smith had the job to backstop a team that could only manage to score 199 goals and win 20 games during the entire season. Even with such a horrible record, Smith still managed to scrape out a decent 3.86 goals-against-average.

81. C. Mario Gosselin

It wasn't his fault, but Mario Gosselin will forever be attached to an unfortunate statistical anomaly. Near the end of a Los Angeles Kings–Edmonton Oilers duel, the Kings netminder Kelly Hrudey was injured late in the third period, and backup goaltender Mario Gosselin was called upon to finish out the remaining minutes of the game. The Kings were down 6–5, with time ticking by slowly, and were forced to pull Gosselin to try for the equalizing goal, only to see the Oilers slide the puck into the empty net to take a 7–5 lead. After Gosselin resumed his position in net, the Kings potted a goal to come within one, but it wasn't enough, and the Oilers won the game by a final score of 7–6. Seeing as Gosselin was the goaltender in the books for the Oilers' seventh goal, he was charged with the loss even though he never allowed a single puck in the net.

Questions 82 – 84

82. Who holds the NHL record for most wins by a rookie goaltender?

A. Patrick Roy

B. Terry Sawchuk

C. Ken Dryden

D. Billy Smith

83. Which goaltender holds the record for most wins in one NHL season?

A. Martin Brodeur

B. Patrick Roy

C. Ken Dryden

D. Bernie Parent

84. Against what team did Patrick Roy play his last game as a member of the Montréal Canadiens on December 2, 1995?

A. Detroit Red Wings

B. Toronto Maple Leafs

C. Buffalo Sabres

D. Chicago Blackhawks

82. B. Terry Sawchuk

The Detroit Red Wings Terry Sawchuk enjoyed great confidence from head coach Tommy Ivan in his first year with the club, playing in all 70 games. The 1950–51 Red Wings enjoyed one of their greatest seasons in the history of their club, thanks to the heroic efforts of the young Sawchuk. His unorthodox style and lightning quick reflexes helped pile up win after win for the rookie, who also recorded a league leading 11 shutouts. The Red Wings didn't win the Cup, but Sawchuk returned the following season and completely dominated the league.

83. A. Martin Brodeur

Until recently, Bernie Parent had held the record for most wins in one season with 47, but another Québecois goaltender by the name of Martin Brodeur of the New Jersey Devils came along in 2006–07 and just beat out Parent with 48 wins. Playing in 78 of the team's 82 games, Brodeur racked up win number 48 on April 5, 2007, in a game against the Philadelphia Flyers in which the Devils won the game by a score of 3–2.

84. A. Detroit Red Wings

That dark day for all Montréal Canadiens fans happened when Patrick Roy was left in the nets for nine goals against the Detroit Red Wings. The Canadiens coach Mario Tremblay and Patrick Roy had never seen eye-to-eye since Tremblay took over the helm, and the tension finally exploded into the now famous incident when Roy was left in net for nine goals. Normally a coach would pull a goalie after five or six goals, sometimes less. After Roy was finally pulled out of the game, he walked over to team President Ronald Corey and told him that he had played his last game as a member of the Montréal Canadiens.

85. **Who was the first goaltender to lose a hundred more games than he won?**

   A.   Cesare Maniago

   B.   Gilles Meloche

   C.   Ron Low

   D.   Jim Rutherford

86. **Who holds the modern-day record for shutouts?**

   A.   Dominik Hasek

   B.   Tony Esposito

   C.   Martin Brodeur

   D.   Bernie Parent

87. **Which netminder let in the goal that ended the longest game in NHL history?**

   A.   Lorne Chabot

   B.   Normie Smith

   C.   Cecil "Tiny" Thompson

   D.   Peter Peeters

88. **Which team selected Vladislav Tretiak in the 1983 NHL Entry Draft?**

   A.   Toronto Maple Leafs

   B.   Edmonton Oilers

   C.   Montréal Canadiens

   D.   Detroit Red Wings

85. C. Ron Low

You have to feel sorry for Ron Low. After a relatively successful Junior hockey career, he found himself drafted and traded to some of the worst teams in the NHL. The worst years of his career came while he was the netminder for the pitiful 1974–75 Washington Capitals, when he won just 8 games, lost 36 and tied 2. Continuing the farce through several more years of bad teams, Low began to pile up a lot more losses than victories. His pace of defeat was so rapid that by the 1983–84 season, he had racked up his first 100 losses before getting anywhere near 100 wins. Low's best season came in 1981–82 when he played in 29 games for the Edmonton Oilers, winning 17, losing 7, with one tie.

86. B. Tony Esposito

Tony Esposito tallied 15 shutouts during his rookie season with the Chicago Blackhawks in 1969–70. The record is separated from the old time record set by George Hainsworth at 22 shutouts, because of the many changes that have affected the way the game is played.

87. A. Lorne Chabot

After six overtime periods, it is hard to blame Chabot for letting in the goal that ended the longest game in the history of the NHL. After the fifth overtime period in the first round of the 1936 Stanley Cup playoffs between the Montréal Maroons and the Detroit Red Wings, game officials actually thought of ending the game and playing at another date because fans had begun to fall asleep in the stands. At 2:00 AM, the hockey radio announcer even began to joke that the arena staff should be providing beds for the bewildered fans. At the two-minute mark of the sixth overtime period, Chabot let out a juicy rebound of a Hec Kilrea shot that found its way onto the stick of Detroit's Modere "Mud" Bruneteau, who simply tapped in the puck for the game-winning goal. Chabot made 68 saves in 176.5 minutes of play.

88. C. Montréal Canadiens

Growing up in Russia, Vladislav Tretiak had always dreamed of one day playing in the NHL for the Montréal Canadiens, but because the Soviet Union was not exactly the best friend of the West, he was barred from ever playing in North America. In a show of defiance, Tretiak made himself available for selection in the 1983 NHL Entry Draft and was selected 143rd overall by the Montréal Canadiens, but because of Soviet regulations, he never got his chance to play in the NHL.

89. Name the only goaltender to register a goals-against-average below 1.00.

A.   Alex Connell

B.   Georges Vezina

C.   Terry Sawchuk

D.   George Hainsworth

90. On December 6, 1995, Patrick Roy was traded to the Colorado Avalanche in return for Andrei Kovalenko, Martin Rucinsky and Jocelyn Thibault. Who was the other member of the Canadiens sent to the Avalanche in the trade?

A.   Kirk Muller

B.   Guy Carbonneau

C.   Mike Keane

D.   Andrew Cassels

91. Who recorded the first shutout in NHL history?

A.   Georges Vezina

B.   Hap Holmes

C.   Hugh Lehman

D.   Clint Benedict

89. D. George Hainsworth

George Hainsworth finished the 1928–29 NHL season with a record-setting goals-against-average of 0.92. That same season, the Montréal Canadiens goaltender recorded another record of 22 shutouts, but all that great goaltending could not save the Canadiens from getting eliminated by the Boston Bruins in the first round of the playoffs.

90. C. Mike Keane

Mike Keane was lucky enough to get shipped out along with Patrick Roy in 1995, because at the end of the season, the Colorado Avalanche won the Stanley Cup.

91. A. Georges Vezina

Georges Vezina got the first shutout in the NHL against the Toronto Arenas 9–0 on February 18, 1918.

92. **Which famous writer stepped in the crease for five minutes of an official NHL exhibition game?**

A. George Plimpton

B. Red Fisher

C. Stephen Leacock

D. Leonard Cohen

93. **Who is the only goaltender to record more shutouts than the rest of the league goaltenders combined?**

A. Frank McCool

B. Johnny Mowers

C. Gump Worsley

D. Bill Durnan

94. **Which team did Tony Esposito start his career with?**

A. Chicago Blackhawks

B. St. Louis Blues

C. Philadelphia Flyers

D. Montréal Canadiens

92. A. George Plimpton

Prior to the start of the 1977–78 regular season, renowned writer George Plimpton approached the Boston Bruins organization and asked if he could play in nets as the Bruins goaltender. Plimpton was already well known for taking up difficult spots in professional sports just to get a good story, having already spent time as the quarterback for the Detroit Lions, which he turned into the best-seller *Paper Lion*. The Bruins agreed and dressed the lanky author in some goal pads and put him nets for an exhibition game against the tough Philadelphia Flyers. Plimpton's stint in goal was highlighted by a save on a penalty shot. He later wrote about the people and his experiences in his best-selling book *Open Net*.

93. B. Johnny Mowers

Unlikely to ever occur again, Detroit Red Wing goaltender Johnny Mowers was the premiere goaltender in the league during the years when most of the talented players were off fighting in World War II. For the 1942–43 season, Mowers recorded just six shutouts, but they were enough to put him past all the goaltenders who managed just five total shutouts. Mowers, of course, won the Vezina Trophy that year and helped lead his team to the Stanley Cup. The following year Mowers joined the military, and when he returned, he could never regain his prior form and never won another game in the NHL.

94. D. Montréal Canadiens

When Tony Esposito began his career with the Montréal Canadiens, the team already had veteran goaltender Gump Worsley and Rogie Vachon between the pipes and a young prospect named Ken Dryden waiting in the wings. During the 1968–69 season, Esposito only got to play 13 games for the Canadiens but still managed to get his name on the Stanley Cup that year despite not playing a single minute in the playoffs. In the off-season he was traded to the Chicago Blackhawks, where he went on to a brilliant career.

95. Name the first goaltender to wear "00" on his jersey.

A.   Brian Hayward

B.   Rejean Lemelin

C.   Mike Liut

D.   Martin Biron

96. Who was the last goaltender to play every minute of every game during one season?

A.   Terry Sawchuk

B.   Jacques Plante

C.   Ed Johnston

D.   Harry Lumley

97. What was goaltender Bill Durnan best known for?

A.   The only goaltender assistant captain

B.   Being ambidextrous

C.   The first goalie to wear a jock

D.   His acrobatic style

95. D. Martin Biron

Although Martin Biron only played three games in the 1995–96 season, he made history as the last goaltender to ever wear "00" on his jersey. Just a few years later, the NHL banned all players from ever wearing the number.

96. C. Ed Johnston

The 1963–64 Boston Bruins were a bad hockey club. Ed Johnston had the unfortunate job of guarding the nets for the Bruins that season, but despite all the losses, Johnston played in every minute of every game. No goaltender since then has played every minute of every game.

97. B. Being ambidextrous

A talented athlete, Bill Durnan added to his goaltending skills early on in his life when he learned how to catch the puck or to hold his stick with either hand. His ambidextrous skills were learned as a kid in Toronto playing in a church league. This unique gift came in handy through-out his playing career, as he able to confuse shooters simply by switching his stick to the other hand.

98. Name the only goaltender to score a game-winning goal.

A. Ron Hextall

B. Jose Theodore

C. Martin Brodeur

D. Evgeni Nabakov

99. Who collected over 400 stitches to his face during his goaltending career?

A. Johnny Bower

B. Terry Sawchuk

C. Gerry Cheevers

D. Jacques Plante

100. Which team did Dave Dryden play for when he played against the Montréal Canadiens and his brother Ken in 1971?

A. New York Rangers

B. Chicago Blackhawks

C. Buffalo Sabres

D. Edmonton Oilers

98. C. Martin Brodeur

Martin Brodeur scored two goals in his career because of his excellent ability to handle the puck, but it was a game winner that gave him this record. He scored the milestone goal in the third period of a game against the Philadelphia Flyers on February 15, 2000. Brodeur was simply the last New Jersey Devils player to touch the puck that Flyer Daymond Langkow accidentally put into his own net. The goal stood as the winner in the Devils' eventual 4–2 victory.

99. B. Terry Sawchuk

Terry Sawchuk is known as one of the greatest goaltenders in the history of the game, but he also has the painful distinction of being one of the most bandaged netminders ever. To know what kind of goaltender Terry Sawchuk was, you just have to find a photo from the March 4, 1966, edition of *Life* magazine. In the magazine there is a close-up portrait of Sawchuk's approximately 400 stitches on his face, which he had received over a career as a netminder without wearing a facemask. Although the scars were enhanced with make-up for photographic effect, each one of the 400 stitches tells the story of the price he paid to stop all those pucks. Part of the reason why he had so many scars was his style of goaltending. By crouching low with his glove and blocker at the ready, Sawchuk was able to get a better view of the ice, allowing him to make quick-reaction saves and lateral moves much faster than the stand up goaltenders.

100. C.   Buffalo Sabres

In the history of the NHL, many brothers have played on the same or opposite teams, but never had there been a game in which two brothers played against each other in goal. That is, until March 20, 1971, when Dave Dryden of the Buffalo Sabres got to play in goal against his younger brother Ken of the Montréal Canadiens. Both goaltenders were not slated to play in nets that night, but when the Canadiens Rogie Vachon went down with an injury, Ken Dryden was put in nets, and Sabres head coach Punch Imlach immediately put Dave in nets. As the two brothers skated out onto the ice, the crowd cheered the historic event. "We were having a hamburger and kind of joked with each other, 'See you at centre ice after we play tomorrow, ha, ha,'" said Dave Dryden. "It was really one of those unbelievable things. Our dad, who took the chance of driving to Montréal when it made no sense, was rewarded."

The younger brother ended up winning the game, but all that didn't matter when the two met at centre ice and shook hands after the game. For the first time since they were kids, the Dryden brothers had played a game of hockey together.

Chapter Five

Those Amazing Hockey Players

---

101. **Who was the only player to ever be named all three stars at the end of a game?**

A. Wayne Gretzky

B. Bobby Hull

C. Jean Beliveau

D. Maurice Richard

102. **Who holds the record for most points in one game?**

A. Mario Lemieux

B. Gordie Howe

C. Darryl Sittler

D. Wayne Gretzky

103. **In the 1923 Stanley Cup final, who said to a young King Clancy, "Hey kid. Take care of this place till I get back"?**

A. Lionel Hitchman

B. Frank Nighbor

C. Clint Benedict

D. George Boucher

101. D. Maurice Richard

On March 23, 1944, Maurice "The Rocket" Richard scored all of the Montréal Canadiens goals in a 5–1 playoff victory over the Toronto Maple Leafs. After the game, Richard waited in the hall leading to the dressing room of the Montréal Forum for the traditional announcement of the three stars, certain that he would have to wait until the first star was called to hear his name. Much to his surprise and to the thousands of fans gathered at the Forum, Richard was announced as the third star, setting off a chorus of boos from the crowd. Fans began to catch on when Richard was announced as the second star, then the roof almost lifted off when he was named the first star as well. On the announcement of the first star, Richard walked back out onto the ice to receive one of the greatest ovations of his distinguished career.

102. C.   Darryl Sittler

Darryl Sittler had the best night of his hockey career on February 7, 1976. When Sittler's Toronto Maple Leafs met the Boston Bruins that night, few anticipated that by the end of the third period Sittler would have contributed to all of the Leafs' 10 goals. From the outset of the game it was apparent that the Leafs were in control, spending the majority of the time in the Bruins defensive zone. Everything seemed to go Sittler's way that night, as each shot somehow found the back of the net or the open blade of a waiting teammate. After all the smoke had cleared, poor Dave Reece had been the victim of six Sittler goals and four others he had assisted on. Maurice Richard previously held the record with eight points in one game.

103. C.   **Clint Benedict**

In the second game of the Stanley Cup finals, the Ottawa Senators King Clancy became the only person in NHL history to play every position in one Stanley Cup game. After playing every position as a player, with just 10 minutes left in the game, Clint Benedict drew a penalty and was forced to sit in the sin bin to serve his time as was the rule during the early years of the game. As Benedict made his way off the ice, King Clancy met him halfway, and Benedict then said, "Hey kid. Take care of this place till I get back."

104. Which player holds the record for the Stanley Cup championships?

A. Red Kelly

B. Jean Beliveau

C. Frank Mahovlich

D. Henri Richard

105. Since Wayne Gretzky was ineligible to win the Calder Trophy in his first season in 1979–80, who won the rookie of the year honours that year?

A. Ray Bourque

B. Peter Stastny

C. Bobby Smith

D. Mark Messier

106. Who was the first player to win the Maurice "Rocket" Richard Trophy?

A. Jaromir Jagr

B. Pavel Bure

C. Teemu Selanne

D. Paul Kariya

104. D. Henri Richard

Playing with the Montréal Canadiens from 1955 to 1975, Henri Richard won a record 11 Stanley Cup championships. Only one other player in all professional North American sport has achieved the same level of success: Bill Russell of the National Basketball Association's Boston Celtics. The Montréal Canadiens Jean Beliveau comes in a close second, winning 10 Stanley Cups in his long career.

105. A. Ray Bourque

If Gretzky had not played one season in the World Hockey League, which made him ineligible because he had played in a professional league, he surely would have won the rookie of the year, but because Gretzky was off the list, Ray Bourque was the obvious second choice. Playing in all 80 games, the speedy rookie defenceman scored 17 goals, 48 assists and was a consistent defensive presence on the ice.

106. C. Teemu Selanne

The Maurice "Rocket" Richard Trophy has been handed out since 1999, to the player who scores the most goals in a single season. It was first awarded to Teemu Selanne of the Anaheim Mighty Ducks, for scoring 47 goals during the regular season.

107. Who scored the fastest hat trick?

A.   Woody Dumart

B.   Maurice Richard

C.   Ted Lindsay

D.   Bill Mosienko

108. Who did the Montréal Canadiens select first overall in 1971?

A.   Rejean Houle

B.   Murray Wilson

C.   Michel Plasse

D.   Guy Lafleur

109. Maurice Richard was the first person to score 50 goals in 50 games, but who was the second player to achieve this incredible milestone?

A.   Bernie Geoffrion

B.   Bobby Hull

C.   Mike Bossy

D.   Wayne Gretzky

107. D.   Bill Mosienko

On March 23, 1952, the Chicago Blackhawks Bill Mosienko scored three goals in just 21 seconds. Mosienko accomplished this against the New York Rangers netminder Lorne Anderson at the halfway point of the third period. The three quick goals started a late rally by the Blackhawks, who ended up winning the game 7–6.

108. D.   Guy Lafleur

The Montréal Canadiens had to make some deals to secure the number one pick overall in 1971, but Guy Lafleur did not disappoint the organization, putting in over a decade of faithful service and helping the Canadiens to five Stanley Cups.

109. C.   Mike Bossy

Prior to the 1980–81 season, Mike Bossy predicted he would break or tie the old record established by Maurice Richard of 50 goals in 50 games, and despite the pressure, he still managed to accomplish the amazing feat. In the last game and last period possible, Bossy scored twice in the final five minutes of the game to equal the Rocket's record.

110. **Who holds the record for most shots on net in a single season (currently standing in at 550 shots)?**

    A.   Alexander Ovechkin

    B.   Phil Esposito

    C.   Wayne Gretzky

    D.   Jaromir Jagr

111. **Who scored the first hat trick by an NHL player in the Stanley Cup finals?**

    A.   Corb Denneny

    B.   Reg Noble

    C.   Didier Pitre

    D.   Alf Skinner

112. **Who was the first player in the NHL to play in 900 consecutive games?**

    A.   Nicklas Lidstrom

    B.   Gary Unger

    C.   Doug Jarvis

    D.   Glenn Hall

110. B.   Phil Esposito

Phil Esposito shot so many times during the 1970–71 regular season that he scored a then record of 76 goals and 76 assists.

111. D.   Alf Skinner

On March 23, 1918, Alf Skinner of the Toronto Arenas scored the first-ever hat trick by an NHL player in the Stanley Cup finals. Toronto won the game that day and went on to win the first Stanley Cup in NHL history.

112. B.   Gary Unger

You might not know his name, but journeyman centre Gary Unger was the first to play in 900 straight games. He ended his streak playing in 914 straight games. Doug Jarvis would later come along and destroy Unger's record.

113. **Who is the only NHL player to score seven goals in one game?**

A. Wayne Gretzky

B. Mario Lemieux

C. Darryl Sittler

D. Joe Malone

114. **Name the last member of the Chicago Blackhawks to win the scoring title.**

A. Bobby Hull

B. Stan Mikita

C. Ed Litzenberger

D. Pierre Pilote

115. **In what season did Gordie Howe last lead the league in scoring?**

A. 1961–62

B. 1962–63

C. 1964–65

D. 1968–69

113. D.　Joe Malone

Although Frank McGee scored 14 goals during a Stanley Cup game, Joe Malone holds the record for most goals in an NHL game. He scored seven goals as a member of the Québec Bulldogs on January 31, 1920, in a 10–6 victory over the Toronto St. Pats.

114. B.　Stan Mikita

Stan Mikita was the last member of the Chicago Blackhawks to win the scoring championship in 1967–68 when he scored 40 goals and 47 assists.

115. B.　1962–63

The great Gordie Howe, Mr. Hockey himself, had his last great season in 1962–63, leading the Red Wings and the league in scoring. He scored 38 goals and 48 assists for 86 points.

Questions 116 – 118

116. **Which player holds the record for the most consecutive games without a penalty?**

A. Mats Naslund

B. Don Marshall

C. Craig Janney

D. Val Fonteyne

117. **Who is the longest serving captain in NHL history?**

A. Alex Delvecchio

B. Steve Yzerman

C. Jean Beliveau

D. Gordie Howe

118. **Who was the last person to act as both player and coach in the NHL?**

A. Doug Harvey

B. Eddie Gerrard

C. Emile Francis

D. Charles Burns

116. D.　Val Fonteyne

If any player was ever to get the award for nicest guy, it would be Val Fonteyne. From February 28, 1965, to December 1, 1968, he played 185 consecutive games without the referee blowing his whistle at him. In his 820 career games, Fonteyne only received 26 minutes in penalties.

117. B.　Steve Yzerman

From 1984 through to 2006, Steve Yzerman served as captain of the Detroit Red Wings for 22 years.

118. D.　Charles Burns

Just seven years into his NHL career as a player, Charles Burns joined the Minnesota North Stars as a centre and was also named as the team's coach. Burns was the last player/coach in NHL history. He coached himself and his team through 44 games during the 1969–70 season, winning just 10 games, losing 22 and tying 12.

119. **Name the Philadelphia Flyer who instigated a fight with the Montréal Canadiens Claude Lemieux during the pre-game warm-up of game six of the 1987 Wales Conference Finals.**

A. Brad Marsh

B. Ron Hextall

C. Rick Tocchet

D. Ed Hospodar

120. **Who is the youngest player to score an NHL goal?**

A. Sidney Crosby

B. Wayne Gretzky

C. Jordan Staal

D. Bep Guidolin

121. **Which special accomplishment did Mario Lemieux achieve on December 30, 1988, in a game against the New Jersey Devils?**

A. Scored the quickest two goals in NHL history

B. Scored his 500th career goal

C. Scored his 800th career point

D. Scored five goals, five different ways

119. D.   Ed Hospodar

The Montréal Canadiens Shayne Corson and Claude Lemieux had developed a ritual before every game of waiting until every opposing player had left the ice after the pre-game skate so that they could shoot a few pucks into the opposing team's net. On May 14, 1987, Philadelphia Flyers tough guy Ed Hospodar enlisted the services of goaltender Chico Resch to put an end to this obvious insulting ritual. When the whistle blew to end the pre-game skate, Corson and Lemieux waited for the Flyers to leave the ice, but when they saw that Resch and Hospodar were determined to be the last players on the ice, they eventually retreated to the Canadiens dressing room.

Feeling confident that they had stopped the Canadiens' ritual, Hospodar and Resch made their way to their respective dressing rooms. Just as they were about to enter into their dressing rooms, they noticed Corson and Lemieux pop back onto the ice and rush toward the Flyers net. Resch was the first to react, whipping his stick at the puck, but he missed, and Lemieux put the puck in the net. Two seconds later, Hospodar was on the ice, raining down punches on top of

Lemieux. It did not take long for both dressing rooms to get wind of the fight, and the ice of the Montréal Forum quickly became the scene of a brawl. As there were no referees out at the time, the battle raged for over 10 minutes. The only one to get punished was Hospodar, who was suspended for the remainder of the playoffs. The Flyers won the series but lost in the Stanley Cup finals to the Edmonton Oilers.

120. D.   Bep Guidolin

A few weeks shy of celebrating his 17th birthday, Bep Guidolin of the 1942 Boston Bruins set the record for the youngest player to score an NHL goal. In addition, he also became the youngest player to play in the NHL. His milestone marker came on November 24, 1942, against the Chicago Blackhawks goaltender Bert Gardiner. Because of the war, many of the best NHL players were off fighting, so younger replacements had to be found, and in order to fill up their lineup, the Bruins had to call on younger talent.

121. D.   Scored five goals, five different ways

On December 30, 1988, Mario Lemieux scored five goals against the New Jersey Devils. As amazing as a five-goal game is, scoring each goal in a different way is incredible. Lemieux scored a power-play goal, scored when his team was shorthanded, scored even-strength, scored on an empty net, and scored on a penalty shot. No one has equaled or come close to scoring for the complete cycle. That's why he was nicknamed "Mario the Magnificent."

122. **Who holds the record for scoring on the most goaltenders in a career?**

A. Steve Yzerman

B. Brett Hull

C. Wayne Gretzky

D. Chris Chelios

123. **In Mike Bossy's career, in how many seasons did he score 50 or more goals?**

A. Three

B. Five

C. Nine

D. Ten

124. **Which player scored the most points in a playoff year and did not win the Stanley Cup?**

A. Wayne Gretzky

B. Brett Hull

C. Patrick Elias

D. Mario Lemieux

125. **Who was the first NHL player to score over 60 goals in his rookie season?**

A. Mike Bossy

B. Teemu Selanne

C. Wayne Gretzky

D. Sidney Crosby

122. C.   Wayne Gretzky

From 1979 to 1999, Wayne Gretzky scored on 155 goaltenders throughout his entire career.

123. C.   Nine

In Mike Bossy's 10 years in the NHL, he scored 50 or more goals in nine different seasons. In his last season in the NHL before injuries forced him out of the game, he scored 38 goals in 1986–87. His best year was in 1978–79, when he scored 69 goals during the regular season.

124. A.   Wayne Gretzky

Wayne Gretzky scored 15 goals and 25 assists in a losing cause during the 1993 Stanley Cup playoffs. Gretzky carried the Los Angeles Kings through four difficult rounds before finally losing to the Montréal Canadiens in five games in the final.

125. B.   Teemu Selanne

Teemu Selanne of the Winnipeg Jets crushed Mike Bossy's old record of 53 goals for a rookie, scoring 76 goals during the 1992–93 regular season.

Chapter Six

The Blueliners

126. Who was the first defenceman to lead the NHL in scoring?

A. Eddie Shore

B. Paul Coffey

C. Bobby Orr

D. Doug Harvey

127. Name the player who holds the record for the most Norris Trophies as best defenceman in the NHL.

A. Nicklas Lidstrom

B. Doug Harvey

C. Ray Bourque

D. Bobby Orr

128. Which player won the Norris Trophy when it was first awarded in 1954?

A. Doug Harvey

B. Red Kelly

C. Al Arbour

D. Tim Horton

126. C.   Bobby Orr

Bobby Orr became the first defenceman in NHL history to lead the league in scoring when he tallied an incredible 120 points in 1969–70. In 76 games Orr scored 33 goals and had 87 assists, for 120 points overall. In second place that year was fellow teammate Phil Esposito, who stood 21 points back with 99 overall.

127. D.   Bobby Orr

On top of being one of the greatest offensive defenceman in NHL history, Bobby Orr was one of the best defensive defencemen in the league, taking home a record eight Norris Trophies for his contribution to hockey. Coming in a close second is Doug Harvey, whose name appears on seven Norris Trophies.

128. B.   Red Kelly

Red Kelly was the first player to be awarded the Norris Trophy. He finished the 1953–54 regular season with 16 goals and 33 assists.

129. **Which defenceman came within one point of beating Bobby Orr's record of 139 points for a defenceman?**

A.   Ray Bourque

B.   Paul Coffey

C.   Chris Chelios

D.   Brian Leetch

130. **Who was the first defenceman to record a hat trick in a Stanley Cup finals game?**

A.   Paul Coffey

B.   Bobby Orr

C.   Eric Desjardins

D.   Bob Baun

131. **Who holds the record for most career points by a defenceman?**

A.   Raymond Bourque

B.   Brian Leetch

C.   Paul Coffey

D.   Chris Chelios

129. B. Paul Coffey

Paul Coffey of the Edmonton Oilers played almost the same style of game as Bobby Orr. Always an offensive threat, Coffey came within just one point of tying Bobby Orr's record point total for a defenceman with 138 points in the 1985–86 regular season. Coffey finished the season third overall in scoring behind Wayne Gretzky and Mario Lemieux.

130. C. Eric Desjardins

Eric Desjardins of the Montréal Canadiens became the first defenceman in NHL history to score three goals in one game of the Stanley Cup finals when he scored all three Habs goals in a 3–2 victory over the Los Angeles Kings on June 2, 1993. He scored the tying goal with just a few seconds left in the game and then scored the winner on Kelly Hrudey for the hat trick.

131. A. Raymond Bourque

Raymond Bourque holds the record for most career points for a defenceman with 1579 total points. He scored 410 goals and 1169 assists.

132. Name the defenceman who scored a Stanley Cup finals game-winning goal on a broken leg.

A.   Bob Baun

B.   Pierre Pilote

C.   Jacques Laperriere

D.   Leo Boivin

133. Who was the first blue liner to record 500 career points?

A.   Red Kelly

B.   Tim Horton

C.   Bill Gadsby

D.   Doug Harvey

134. Which Toronto defenceman needed 200 stitches to close a gash on his face?

A.   Bob Baun

B.   Borje Salming

C.   Bryan Berard

D.   Bryan McCabe

135. How many defencemen in the history of the NHL have recorded over 100 points?

A.   Two

B.   Three

C.   Five

D.   Six

132. A.   Bob Baun

It's not something that many players can brag about, but Bob Baun of the Toronto Maple Leafs always had a story to tell. The Leafs faced off against the Detroit Red Wings in the 1964 Stanley Cup finals in a bid to win their third Cup in a row, but the Red Wings were making things difficult with a 3–2 series lead.

The Maple Leafs would need 100 percent effort from all their players if they were going to pull off the upset. The score was tied 3–3 in game six in the third period. The Red Wings were pressing the Toronto defence hard, but tough guys Bob Baun and Allen Stanley kept the Wings at Bay. Just seven minutes into the period, Gordie Howe led a Red Wing rush into the Toronto zone and blasted a shot from the blue line toward the goaltender. Unfortunately, the frozen puck found its way in between the unpadded area on defenceman Bob Baun's leg, sending the six footer crashing to the ice. The game was stopped as Baun was carried off the ice on a stretcher, with the pain of having been taken out of the game more apparent on his face than the actual physical pain.

The doctors examined his leg and feared that he might have fractured a bone. When Baun heard that the game had just gone into overtime, he shrugged off the concerns of the doctors, told them to do whatever they could to dull the pain and headed back out onto the ice to help his team. After just a few minutes on the ice, Baun intercepted a Red Wing breakout pass and fired it back into their zone directly at goaltender Terry Sawchuk. Somehow the puck fooled Sawchuk and got past him for the game-winning goal. Baun played game seven with a broken leg, and after the Stanley Cup celebrations, he finally had it x-rayed. It turned out he had a fractured bone above the ankle. Now that is tough!

133. C. Bill Gadsby

On November 4, 1962, the Detroit Red Wings Bill Gadsby became the first defenceman to record a 500th career point. The Hall of Fame defenceman spent several years as the lone shining star with the Chicago Blackhawks, and then with the New York Rangers. Injury threatened to end his career, but the tough blueliner stayed in the game and ended up playing in the league for 20 years before ending his career with the Red Wings with a total of 568 points.

134. B. Borje Salming

People did not think much of Borje Salming when he first entered into the NHL in 1973, but after a few seasons they knew that this tough Swede was one of the premiere players in the league. His toughness became legendary when Gerard Gallant of the Detroit Red Wings accidentally stepped on Salming's face during a game in 1986. Salming needed 200 stitches to close the wound. He was left with a large scar on his face, running from the middle of his forehead to the top of his upper lip.

135. C. Five

Bobby Orr, Denis Potvin, Paul Coffey, Al MacInnis and Brian Leetch are the only defencemen in NHL history to score 100 points or more in a single season. Bobby Orr and Paul Coffey are the only two defencemen to have scored 100 or more points in more than one season; Orr scored 100 points in six consecutive seasons, and Coffey did it in five (nonconsecutive).

136. Who holds the record for most goals in one game by a defenceman?

A. Paul Coffey

B. Ian Turnbull

C. Pierre Pilote

D. Sheldon Souray

137. Paul Coffey shares the record for most points by a defenceman in one game with 8 points with what other NHL defenceman?

A. Ian Turnbull

B. Tom Bladon

C. Bobby Orr

D. Larry Robinson

138. Who won the Norris Trophy in 2000?

A. Scott Niedermayer

B. Chris Pronger

C. Scott Stevens

D. Nicklas Lidstrom

136. B.   Ian Turnbull

Ian Turnbull had the game of his life on February 2, 1977, when he scored five of Toronto's nine goals against the Detroit Red Wings.

137. B.   Tom Bladon

Tom Bladon of the Philadelphia Flyers scored four goals and four assists against the Cleveland Barons on December 11, 1977. The Flyers won the game 11–1.

138. B.   Chris Pronger

St. Louis Blues captain Chris Pronger silenced his many critics by winning the Norris Trophy in 2000. When he first broke into the league, he was immature both on and off the ice and was widely predicted to continue on his downward spiral, but after a few years and some tough love by his coaches, Pronger turned into the leader of the Blues and one of the best defencemen of his time.

139. Who holds the record for the most goals by a defenceman in one Stanley Cup playoff season?

A. Bobby Orr

B. Larry Robinson

C. Paul Coffey

D. Mathieu Schneider

140. Name the last defenceman to win the Conn Smythe Trophy as the most valuable player in the playoffs.

A. Nicklas Lidstrom

B. Scott Stevens

C. Chris Pronger

D. Scott Niedermayer

141. Who was the first defenceman to score 20 goals in one season?

A. Eddie Shore

B. Frank "Flash" Hollett

C. Butch Bouchard

D. Frank Eddolls

139. C. Paul Coffey

Paul Coffey's goal-scoring feats did not stop at the end of the regular season. During the 1984–85 Stanley Cup playoffs, the mobile defenceman scored a defensive record 12 goals as the Oilers went on to win another Stanley Cup championship.

140. D. Scott Niedermayer

Scott Niedermayer proved to be the best player in the 2006–07 Stanley Cup playoffs. His amazing defensive skills and ability to develop an attack helped the Anaheim Ducks defeat the Ottawa Senators in the finals. Before him, Nicklas Lidstrom was the last defenceman to win the Conn Smythe in 2002.

141. B. Frank "Flash" Hollett

Hollett was the first high-scoring mobile defenceman in the league. He almost broke the 20-goal mark twice while playing for the Boston Bruins in 1942 and 1943. Hollett finally broke the mark as a member of the Detroit Red Wings when he scored exactly 20 goals in 50 games during the 1944–45 regular season.

142. Who was James Norris of the Norris Trophy fame?

A. Former owner of the Detroit Red Wings

B. One of the original founders of the NHL

C. One of the best defenceman from the pre-NHL days

D. A mediocre defenceman who died under tragic circumstances

143. Which defenceman almost killed Toronto Maple Leafs star Ace Bailey?

A. Sprague Cleghorn

B. Ching Johnson

C. Eddie Shore

D. Georges Mantha

144. With what team did Scott Stevens begin his career?

A. New Jersey Devils

B. St. Louis Blues

C. Washington Capitals

D. New York Islanders

142. A.   Former owner of the Detroit Red Wings

James Norris was the owner of the Detroit Red Wings from 1932 to 1952. As a young man, Norris played hockey for McGill University and briefly in 1898 for the Montréal Hockey Club, but because he was never considered good enough to go into hockey full time, he entered his father's business. Several decades later, Norris took over the family business and made a small fortune. But he never lost his passion for hockey, and in 1932 he used some money from his businesses to purchase the floundering Detroit Falcons franchise. He immediately changed their name to the Detroit Red Wings. Norris was a constant figure in hockey up until his death in 1954. He was elected to the Hockey Hall of Fame in 1958 for his role as a builder of the game.

143. C.   Eddie Shore

Many people think hockey was a gentleman's game back in the 1920s and 1930s, but the reality is that it was even more bloody and violent than the modern game. To find the perfect example of hockey's original tough guy, look no further than the Boston Bruins Eddie Shore.

Players in the league knew that when entering into the Bruins defensive end, they were taking their chances with their health when Shore was on the ice. But one night in 1933 when the Bruins played the Toronto Maple Leafs, Shore went one step too far.

It was December 12, 1933, when the Bruins played host to the Toronto Maple Leafs. After a rough first period, both teams were deadlocked at one apiece. Eddie Shore was particularly active that night, hitting players in his usual unfriendly manner. Wanting to give Shore a taste of his own medicine, Toronto's King Clancy tripped Shore from behind as he skated out of the Toronto defensive zone. Shore immediately sprang to his feet, burning with rage and looking out for the nearest Leafs jersey to exact his revenge upon. Leafs captain Ace Bailey just happened to be the closest to Shore. Blind with anger, Shore viciously checked Bailey from behind, sending him flying through the air. As Bailey landed, his unprotected head hit the ice with a thud, and he lay sprawled on the ice, out cold. Upon seeing his teammate twitching on the ice, Toronto's Red Horner responded by sending Shore to the ice with one punch to the jaw. When the commotion settled, Bailey was rushed to the hospital where neurosurgeons had to perform two operations in order to repair his broken skull, remove two blood clots and reduce swelling on the brain that would have certainly killed him. Shore received a suspension, and although Bailey would recover, he never played another game.

144. C.   Washington Capitals

The rock solid Scott Stevens began checking bodies with the Washington Capitals. He was selected fifth overall in the 1982 NHL Entry Draft because of his unique offensive talents and his remarkable ability to check opposing players into near oblivion. After playing eight seasons with the Capitals, he signed as a free agent with the St. Louis Blues before moving to the New Jersey Devils, where he ended his career in 2004.

145. **Larry Robinson played the majority of his career with the Montréal Canadiens, but with which team did he end his playing career?**

A. New Jersey Devils

B. New York Rangers

C. Detroit Red Wings

D. Los Angeles Kings

146. **Who holds the lowest plus/minus for a Norris Trophy–winning defenceman?**

A. Denis Potvin (Norris Trophy 1978)

B. Randy Carlyle (Norris Trophy 1981)

C. Rob Blake (Norris Trophy 1998)

D. Paul Coffey (Norris Trophy 1986)

147. **Which team had a defensive corps known as the "Big Three"?**

A. Calgary Flames

B. Boston Bruins

C. New York Islanders

D. Montréal Canadiens

145. D. Los Angeles Kings

After 17 years of faithful service for the Montréal Canadiens, Larry Robinson finished off his career with three more seasons in sunny Los Angeles with the Kings in 1991–92.

146. B. Randy Carlyle (Norris Trophy 1981)

Since the plus/minus system was first introduced in 1967–68, only two defencemen have scored in the negative zones. Randy Carlyle wins this dubious honour, having tallied a rating of –16 the same year he won the 1981 Norris Trophy. Rob Blake is the only other recipient to score in the negatives, with a rating of –3 in 1998.

147. D. Montréal Canadiens

The Montréal Canadiens dynasty of the 1970s relied heavily on their big defensive line of Serge Savard, Larry Robinson and Guy Lapointe. These three players gave the Canadiens the ability to make offensive mistakes and know that the defence would always be there to cover them. All three players were well over 6 feet tall and naturally were nicknamed the "Big Three."

148. **Which goaltender did Bobby Orr score his famous Stanley Cup–winning goal against (the one where he flew through the air after scoring the goal)?**

   A.   Jacques Plante

   B.   Glenn Hall

   C.   Gump Worsley

   D.   Bernie Parent

149. **Bobby Orr holds the current record for most points in one season, established with 139 points in the 1970–71 regular season, but who held the record for most points by a defenceman before him?**

   A.   Allan Stanley

   B.   Red Kelly

   C.   Pierre Pilote

   D.   Tom Johnson

150. **Name the only defenceman and doctor to win the Stanley Cup.**

   A.   Craig Ludwig

   B.   Bill Juzda

   C.   Randy Gregg

   D.   Doug Young

148. B. Glenn Hall

Although Bobby Orr was not the first defenceman to rush into the offensive zone with the puck, he was the first to use his offensive skills on a regular basis and with such outstanding success. By combining solid defensive skills with his flamboyant offensive rushes, Orr was one of the most dangerous players on the ice. The St. Louis Blues and their goaltender Glenn Hall learned this fact firsthand during the 1970 Stanley Cup finals. The Bruins were the far superior team and easily won the first three games of the series. In game four, however, the St. Louis Blues decided to go down fighting, and by the end of the third period, the score was tied and headed into overtime.

What happened next is one of the most memorable moments in hockey history. The winning play began with a brilliant pass from the Bruins tough guy Derek Sanderson. Spotting Orr sneaking in from the point, Sanderson shot him a quick pass. Suddenly Orr was in front of goaltender Glenn Hall. Orr skated across the front of the net, forcing Hall to commit to a shot prematurely, and Orr was able to slide the puck underneath the sprawled-out goaltender. Blues defenceman

Noel Picard tried to stop Orr but was a fraction of a second too late. As Orr's shot hit the back of the net, Picard lifted Orr's skates into the air and sent him flying across the crease. Overcome with emotion at having scored the winning goal in the Stanley Cup finals, Orr raised his arms in triumph as he flew through the air, seemingly unaware that the ice was quickly rushing up at him. At that precise instant, a photographer snapped off a shot and captured the moment perfectly. "Seeing the famous photograph of me flying through the air after scoring the overtime goal to give the Boston Bruins the 1970 Stanley Cup brings back a flood of memories," said Orr in the book *For the Love of Hockey*. "I remember the thrill of getting that goal and the good fortune of being part of that special team. When I was a boy, I watched in awe as the Stanley Cup was carried high over the shoulders of the winning team, and today, that photograph represents the excitement of realizing that dream."

Glenn Hall recalled that moment with a hint of sarcasm. "I always tell Bobby he was up in the air for so long that I had time to shower and change before he hit the ice."

149. C. Pierre Pilote

Before the arrival of Bobby Orr into the NHL, Pierre Pilote was the premiere offensive defence-man in the league. The Chicago Blackhawks defenceman and captain was excellent at moving forward with the puck, and he has three Norris Trophies to his name to prove it.

In 1964–65, Pilote scored 14 goals and 45 assists for 59 points in 68 games. Then along came Bobby Orr, who scored 64 points in 1968–69 to break the record. Just a few years later, Orr set the mark very high for all future defencemen, scoring 139 points in 1970–71.

150. C. Randy Gregg

When Randy Gregg won his first of five Stan-ley Cups with the Edmonton Oilers, he became the first defenceman and doctor to win the Stan-ley Cup. Dr. Randy Gregg earned his medical degree in Japan before returning to Canada and signing with the Oilers. The first player and doctor to win the Cup was Rod Smylie of the Toronto St. Pats in 1922.

Chapter Seven

True or False?

---

151. Maurice Richard was suspended in 1955 because he was French.

True or False?

152. Wayne Gretzky's first point in the NHL was an assist.

True or False?

153. The Philadelphia Flyers Rick MacLeish was the first player from an expansion team to score 50 goals.

True or False?

154. Roy Worters was the tallest goaltender ever to play the game.

True or False?

151. False

Some diehard Montréal Canadiens fans would argue this one. It was widely known that league president Clarence Campbell was not the biggest fan of French Canadians and that he particularly disliked Richard, but the main reason for Richard's suspension just before the start of the 1955 playoffs was an incident that occurred during a game against the Boston Bruins. Richard had a laundry list of incidents during his career long before the suspension of 1955, but as Clarence Campbell put it, giving him a fine really didn't matter much: "For every $250 I fined him, Québec businessmen would send him $1000. Richard could do no wrong in Québec. I was always the villain." The final straw came during a game against the Boston Bruins on March 13, 1955. By the third period of the game, both teams were well bruised from very physical play. The incident that got Richard suspended happened late in the third period when Boston defenceman Hal Laycoe and Richard both rushed into the corner after the puck and collided with a tangle of arms and sticks.

Richard got the worst of the collision. As he fell to the ice, his stick caught Laycoe on the head, creating a gash that poured blood all over

Laycoe's jersey. Furious at the assault, Laycoe swung his stick at Richard several times, catching him on the side of the head. Blood trickled down Richard's face and into his eyes. When he saw the blood, he lost his temper. His eyes changed from cold black to fire red, with a sole objective—to hurt Laycoe. The two players were out to kill each other. Hoping to stop the fight was linesman Cliff Thompson, who jumped in and tried several times to hold Richard back, but the Rocket was so enraged that Thompson could not stop him. Richard warned the linesman to leave him alone. Thompson did not listen and grabbed Richard once more, this time grabbing his arm and pinning it behind him. Laycoe, seeing that Richard was being held back, jumped on the opportunity and punched Richard several times. Luckily, a fellow teammate pushed Laycoe out of the way, giving Richard an opportunity to break free from Thompson's grasp. Richard seized his chance, turned around and punched the linesman twice in the face. "He wouldn't listen. That's why I hit him," said Richard.

What is often omitted from the story is that Cliff Thompson had at one time been a defenceman for the Boston Bruins. Whether this was a factor in his holding Richard back is not known, but it is interesting to note that Thompson did not officiate another game in the NHL. Richard received a suspension for the remainder of the season and for the playoffs. Without Richard's help, the Canadiens lost in the Stanley Cup finals to the Detroit Red Wings in seven games. Many Canadiens fans still to this day blame Clarence Campbell for taking away the Habs' chance at six straight Stanley Cups.

152. True

In his first game in the NHL on October 10, 1979, Wayne Gretzky assisted on a goal by Kevin Lowe against the Chicago Blackhawks.

153. True

At the end of the 1972–73 season, the Philadelphia Flyers Rick MacLeish became the first expansion team player to score 50 goals when he compiled 50 goals and 50 assists for 100 points.

154. False

Roy Worters was the shortest player in the history of the NHL. Despite his small stature, Worters was one of the top goaltenders of his time. And had he played on more successful teams, history might have given him more credit than he has received.

Questions 155 – 160

155. **Cy Young Award–winning pitcher Tom Glavine was selected in the second round by the Winnipeg Jets in 1984.**

    True or False?

156. **On June 5, 2006, Chris Pronger of the Edmonton Oilers became the only player in the history of the NHL to score on a penalty shot in the Stanley Cup finals.**

    True or False?

157. **Wayne Gretzky was selected number one overall in the 1979 Expansion Draft.**

    True or False?

158. **Joe Malone holds the record for the most goals-per-game average over a entire NHL season.**

    True or False?

159. **Martin Brodeur has only one Conn Smythe Trophy under his belt.**

    True or False?

160. **Before 1929, forward passing outside the defensive zone was not allowed.**

    True or False?

155. True

Not only is he one of the best pitchers in baseball, but before Tom Glavine ever put on an
Atlanta Braves uniform, he was also one of the
top prospects in hockey. In his senior year in
high school he was selected as player of the year
after scoring 44 goals and 41 assists. His hockey
skills were good enough to get him drafted 69th
overall by the Los Angeles Kings in the 1984
NHL Entry Draft. As if that wasn't enough, he
was also selected that same year in the second
round by the Atlanta Braves in the Major League
Baseball Draft. But it was baseball that he truly
loved, "I just felt, being a left handed pitcher
I had a little better chance of making it to major
leagues in baseball."

156. True

Hard to believe, but big defenceman Chris
Pronger became the only player in NHL history
to score on a penalty shot when he put the puck
past Carolina Hurricanes goaltender Cam Ward
in game one of the finals.

157. False

Gretzky was never drafted, because he had played one year in the World Hockey Association professional league, effectively making him ineligible for the NHL Entry Draft.

158. True

While most would believe that Wayne Gretzky's 92 goals in 80 games during the 1981–82 season would give him the record, Joe Malone's 44 goals in 20 games wins this hockey statistics record. While Gretzky's average works out to an impressive 1.15 goals per game, Malone tops them all with an average of 2.2 goals per game. But, of course, could Malone have kept up that scoring pace over a full 80-game schedule?

159. False

Martin Brodeur never won a Conn Smythe Trophy. Despite leading his team to three Stanley Cups, Brodeur goaltending heroics were overshadowed by Claude Lemieux in 1995, Scott Stevens in 2000 and by goaltending opponent Jean-Sebastien Giguere of the Anaheim Mighty Ducks in 2003.

160. True

Before 1929, goaltenders dominated the game. In the 1928–29 season, George Hainsworth was the top goaltender recording 22 shutouts. No forward passing in the offensive zones made it difficult for a team to enter into an opponent's defensive zone. It also meant low scoring and bored fans, so before the start of the 1929–30 season, the league changed the rules to allow forward passing, and the difference was immediate. The top scorer before the rule change was Ace Bailey with 22 goals and 10 assists. Just one season later, Cooney Weiland of the Bruins scored 43 goals and 30 assists. Hockey was once again an exciting affair.

Questions 161 – 165

161. **The Stanley Cup was originally purchased for $50.**

   True or False?

162. **The Toronto Maple Leafs Bunny Larocque holds the record for allowing the most goals in a single period (currently holding at nine goals).**

   True or False?

163. **Gordie Howe won five Stanley Cups.**

   True or False?

164. **No NHL hockey team has ever put the image of a woman on their jerseys.**

   True or False?

165. **The Montréal Canadiens selected Ken Dryden 14th overall in the 1964 NHL Draft.**

   True or False?

Answers 161 – 165

161. True

Ever since Canada's Governor General Lord Stanley purchased the Dominion Hockey Challenge Cup for about $50 in 1892, hockey players from all over the world have made it their life-long ambition just to hold it. Prior to the Stanley Cup, there was no individual trophy that hockey players from across Canada could compete for, so Lord Stanley offered up his trophy. Although the original Cup was only 18 centimetres high, with the diminutive Cup, Lord Stanley started one of the greatest traditions in sports. Its name, the Dominion Hockey Challenge Cup, was shortened to the "Stanley Cup" after Montréal's AAAs won it for the first time in 1893. Lord Stanley best put the need for the Cup in his own words in a letter to a friend:

I have for some time been thinking that it would be a good thing if there were a challenge cup which should be held from year to year by the champion hockey team in the Dominion [of Canada].

There does not appear to be any such outward sign of a championship at present, and considering the general interest which matches now elicit, and the importance of having the game played fairly and under rules generally recognized, I am willing to give a cup which shall be held from year to year by the winning team.

162. True

Bunny Larocque joined the Toronto Maple Leafs in 1981 from the Montréal Canadiens. His goaltending skills were expected to bring the Leafs back from the basement of the league, but just nine days after the trade, Larocque experienced the worst period of his or any other goaltender's life. On March 19, 1981, when the Leafs met the Buffalo Sabres, Larocque was scored on a total of nine times in the second period of a blowout 14–4 game. Just three years later, Larocque retired from the game.

163. False

After 26 seasons in the NHL, Gordie Howe won just four Stanley Cup championships. Hard to imagine after such a long, distinguished career that Mr. Hockey did not win more than that.

164. False

When the New York Rangers wanted to add a third jersey, they decided to have a symbol that represented perfectly what New York was all about. After an exhaustive search for the right symbol, the Rangers settled on the image of Old Lady Liberty for their jerseys. The new jerseys were unveiled for the 1996–97 season. "We wanted a look that was identifiable with New York, and the Statue of Liberty was a better choice than, say, the Empire State Building," said Rangers General Manager Neil Smith.

165. False

It was the Boston Bruins who selected Ken Dryden in the 1964 NHL Amateur Draft. His rights were later traded away to the Canadiens in return for two players whose names people only remember because they were traded for the Hall of Fame goaltender.

166. **Terry Sawchuk died of a heart attack.**

     True or False?

167. **Maurice Richard never won the scoring tile.**

     True or False?

168. **The Toronto Maple Leafs were one of the original teams that opened up the NHL in 1917.**

     True or False?

169. **The Montréal Canadiens won the Stanley Cup in 1919.**

     True or False?

170. **Ilya Kovalchuk was the first Russian-trained player drafted number one overall in the NHL Entry Draft.**

     True or False?

166. False

After 400 stitches to the face and a long list of injuries, you might think that Terry Sawchuk would live forever after facing down some of the biggest, fastest and toughest athletes in the world. A heart attack would seem a probable cause of death for the high-strung goaltender, but Sawchuk died under more unusual circumstances. Unfortunately, Sawchuk's career did not end with the big ceremony he deserved. Instead of ending a career filled on a high note, it ended with a sombre memorial to a life taken too soon. Playing for the New York Rangers at the time, after the team was eliminated from the 1970 playoffs, Sawchuk was involved in a scuffle with teammate Ron Stewart over who would clean the home they shared. Although it remains unclear as to the actual circumstances of what happened, during the altercation, apparently Sawchuk fell and sustained internal injuries. Paramedics arrived on the scene and rushed the goaltender to the hospital.

For a healthy person, the injuries would have meant only a routine hospital visit, but for the weatherworn goaltender who was plagued by injuries, ill health and years of hard drinking, it meant several major operations and a lengthy stay under the watchful eye of doctors. But the trauma was too much for Sawchuk, and on May 31, 1970, at the age of 40, he died in his sleep from a blood clot in his lungs. Regardless of how his life ended, Terry Sawchuk is remembered as one of the greatest goaltenders to take to the ice.

167. True

Despite all his amazing achievements, Maurice "the Rocket" Richard never managed to win the scoring title. Even the year he became the first person to score 50 goals in one season, he missed the top scoring spot by a few points. He came the closest in the 1954–55 season, but because of his suspension for punching out a referee, Richard missed the last few games and was beat out for the scoring title by fellow teammate Bernie Geoffrion by a single point.

168. False

Technically, it has been the same Toronto franchise since 1917, but they weren't named the Toronto Maple Leafs until Conn Smythe took over during the 1926–27 regular season.

169. False

Although the Montréal Canadiens did make it into the Stanley Cup finals in 1919 against the Seattle Metropolitans, no champion was named because the Spanish Influenza had ravaged most of the team, killing one player.

170. True

By the year 2000, Russian hockey players had become a staple on most teams in the NHL. It was just a matter of time before one of the skilled players from Russia's talented leagues got the top billing. When Ilya Kovalchuk was selected first overall in the 2001 NHL Entry Draft by the Atlanta Thrashers, he became the first Russian to go number one overall.

Questions 171 – 175

171. At one time in the league, when a player received a two-minute penalty, he had to sit out the entire two minutes even if the opposing team scored a goal.

    True or False?

172. During the early days of hockey, in the playoffs, NHL teams played games with seven players on the ice.

    True or False?

173. Mario Lemieux was always being compared to Wayne Gretzky, so when he joined the NHL he wore the number 66 because it was 99 upside down.

    True or False?

174. The New York Americans played the first-ever game in Madison Square Garden.

    True or False?

175. The Montréal Canadiens are the oldest team in NHL history.

    True or False?

171. True

Before the 1955–56 NHL season, when a player was assessed a minor penalty, he had to sit out his punishment for the entire two minutes regardless if the opposing team scored a goal. This meant that the opposing team was free to score as many goals as they could in that two-minute period. The rule was changed when the high-scoring Montréal Canadiens, at the beginning of their 1950s dynasty, used the minor power-play rule to their advantage. The league decided to change the rule after one particular game on November 5, 1955, when the Canadiens played to a 4–2 victory over the Boston Bruins. The Bruins were leading early on in the game by a score of 2–1 when a Bruins player was called for a two-minute minor penalty. This is when scoring ace Jean Beliveau scored three goals in 44 seconds to put the Canadiens in the lead. At the end of the season, the poor defensive teams protested, and the rule was changed so that after a goal was scored during a minor penalty, the penalized team could return to full strength.

172. True

Because the Stanley Cup was not the official property of the NHL until 1926, the league had to play teams from the pro-leagues in the West who still played under the seven-man system. The teams usually alternated between the NHL six-man system and the West's seven-man system.

173. True

Coming up through the minors, Mario Lemieux was constantly being compared with Wayne Gretzky. Even if they played completely different styles of hockey, the media loved to compare the two players, so Lemieux changed his number to 66, which is 99 upside down.

174. True

Joining the NHL for the 1925–26 season, the New York Americans played host to the Montréal Canadiens in the first-ever NHL game played in Madison Square Garden. The Canadiens beat the Americans by a score of 3–1.

175. True (and a little False)

The Montréal Canadiens began operations in 1909 in the now defunct National Hockey Association and have continued to thrive for almost a century. However, the Ottawa Senators were one of the first professional teams in Canada, beginning operations in 1884, but the club did not exist from 1934 to 1992, so the Montréal Canadiens retain their title as the oldest team in the NHL.

Chapter Eight

There Is No "I" In Team

---

176. Name the only team to come back from a 3–0 series deficit and win in the Stanley Cup finals.

A.   Montréal Canadiens

B.   Detroit Red Wings

C.   Boston Bruins

D.   Toronto Maple Leafs

177. Name the only other team to come back from a 3–0 series deficit in the Stanley Cup playoffs.

A.   New York Rangers

B.   New York Islanders

C.   Edmonton Oilers

D.   Calgary Flames

178. Name the team the Montréal Canadiens beat to win their fifth Stanley Cup Championship in a row.

A.   Detroit Red Wings

B.   Boston Bruins

C.   New York Rangers

D.   Toronto Maple Leafs

176. D.   Toronto Maple Leafs

In the 1942 Stanley Cup finals, the Toronto Maple Leafs had dug themselves a considerable hole by losing the first three games of the Stanley Cup finals to the Detroit Red Wings. But Leafs head coach Hap Day would not let his players give up, and Toronto slowly started climbing back in the series. His players fought hard and were rewarded in the seventh game when Leafs forward Pete Langelle scored the game-winning goal and Sweeney Schriner scored the insurance goal to give the Leafs a 3–1 victory and take the championship.

177. B.   New York Islanders

The 1975 New York Islanders are the only other team to come back from a 3–0 series deficit when they bounced back against the Pittsburgh Penguins in the Stanley Cup quarterfinals. They almost repeated the feat in the next round against the Philadelphia Flyers but could not win in game seven.

178. D.   Toronto Maple Leafs

The Canadiens beat the Toronto Maple Leafs in a four-game sweep to win a record five Stanley Cup championships in a row.

179. Which NHL arena was the first to install a suspended time clock?

A. The Montréal Forum

B. Boston Gardens

C. Madison Square Gardens

D. Maple Leaf Gardens

180. Which expansion team made it into the Stanley Cup finals three years in a row and lost each one?

A. Minnesota North Stars

B. St. Louis Blues

C. Philadelphia Flyers

D. Buffalo Sabres

181. Which team has gone the longest without winning the Stanley Cup?

A. Toronto Maple Leafs

B. St. Louis Blues

C. Chicago Blackhawks

D. Boston Bruins

179. D.   Maple Leaf Gardens

It wasn't until 1931 that the Maple Leaf Gardens became the first arena in the NHL to use the centre-ice-mounted suspended clock. Widely referred to as the "Player's Please," because of the large cigarette ad, the clock was one of the most recognizable features in the Gardens until it was changed in 1967 in favour of a larger and more up-to-date version.

180. B.   St. Louis Blues

Despite their expansion status, the 1967 to 1970 St. Louis Blues made it into the Stanley Cup finals three years in a row and lost each time. When the league expanded operations in 1967, it bunched the new teams into the West Division, leaving the established original six teams to fight it out in the East Division. This separation resulted in a severe imbalance of power between the two divisions and made it easier for a decent team from the West to completely dominate over the other expansion teams. Plus it didn't hurt to have legendary goaltenders Jacques Plante and Glenn Hall in nets and a young upstart coach named Scotty Bowman calling the shots. With excellent goaltending and intelligent coaching, the St. Louis Blues made it all the way to the finals three times, losing twice to the Montréal Canadiens and once to the Boston Bruins.

181. C.   Chicago Blackhawks

Since last winning the Stanley Cup in 1961, the Chicago Blackhawks organization has gone 46 years without a championship. Although coming close on several occasions, the Black-hawks have not been able to get that one extra win to put them over the top. (They lost the 1971 Stanley Cup finals to the Montréal Canadiens in the seventh game by just one goal.) The Toronto Maple Leafs take the second spot on this dubious list, having not won the Cup since 1967.

Questions 182 – 184

182. **Name the only team to have four of its players finish first through fourth in scoring by the end of the regular season.**

   A.   Boston Bruins

   B.   Montréal Canadiens

   C.   Chicago Blackhawks

   D.   Edmonton Oilers

183. **Which team was the last one to put names on the backs of their jerseys?**

   A.   Toronto Maple Leafs

   B.   Boston Bruins

   C.   Detroit Red Wings

   D.   Montréal Canadiens

184. **Name the last non-NHL team to win the Stanley Cup.**

   A.   Seattle Metropolitans

   B.   Vancouver Millionaires

   C.   Victoria Cougars

   D.   Edmonton Eskimos

182. A.   Boston Bruins

The 1970–71 and 1973–74 Boston Bruins were the highest-scoring teams of the 1970s. Led by defenceman Bobby Orr and power forward Phil Esposito, the Bruins had a plethora of scoring talent. During those years, four of their players finished first through to fourth, the only team to have four players finish at the top. In 1970–71, the four Bruin players were, in order, Phil Esposito with 152 points, Bobby Orr with 139 points, Johnny Bucyk with 116 points and Ken Hodge with 105 points. In 1973–74, the four players were, in order, Phil Esposito with 145 points, Bobby Orr with 122 points, Ken Hodge with 105 points and Wayne Cashman with 89 points.

183. A. Toronto Maple Leafs

When the league made it mandatory to have players' names on jerseys in 1978, several teams had already put names on the backs of jerseys, but the Toronto Maple Leafs held out against the ruling as long as they could. Pugnacious owner Harold Ballard did not want names on the team's home jerseys because he felt it would hurt existing sales. He was able to circumvent the new rule because he had a contract with a jersey manufacturer that he said could not be broken until the following season.

184. C.   Victoria Cougars

Before the Stanley Cup became the sole property of the NHL, the Victoria Cougars of the Western Canadian Hockey League were the last team from a league other than the NHL to win the Stanley Cup. Facing off against the Montréal Canadiens in the 1925 playoffs in Victoria, BC, the Cougars were the far superior team. Although the Canadiens had the likes of Howie Morenz, Aurel Joliat and the goaltending of Georges Vezina, the Cougars were stacked with veteran talent such as goaltender Harry "Hap" Holmes, forward Frank Foyston and the brilliant mind of head coach and hockey legend Frank Patrick. The Canadiens put up a decent fight in the best-of-five series, but they could only manage to get one win as the Cougars won the series three games to one. The Cougars made it back into the Stanley Cup finals the following year, but it was the Montréal Maroons that outclassed them this time, beating them three games to one.

185. How many overtime wins did the Montréal Canadiens rack up on their road to the 1993 Stanley Cup championship?

A. 6

B. 8

C. 10

D. 12

186. In what year did the Toronto Maple Leafs win their first Stanley Cup?

A. 1929

B. 1931

C. 1932

D. 1942

187. Name one of the only two teams to lose at least 70 games in a single season.

A. Tampa Bay Lighting

B. Columbus Blue Jackets

C. Winnipeg Jets

D. Ottawa Senators

185. C.   10

The Montréal Canadiens strung together an amazing 10 straight overtime victories in the 1993 Stanley Cup playoffs on their way to winning their 24th franchise Stanley Cup, but their lucky run did not start off well. In the first round against the Québec Nordiques, the Canadiens lost the first game of the series in overtime, but for the rest of the playoffs, the Habs proved to be masters of sudden-death overtime. They strung together two more overtime victories against the Nordiques on their way into the division finals against the Buffalo Sabres. The Canadiens then continued their magic with the Sabres, winning three straight of the four games in overtime by the identical score of 4–3 each time. Next, against the New York Islanders, the Canadiens added two more overtime victories before moving on to the Stanley Cup finals versus the Los Angeles Kings. Head coach Jacques Demers knew that something special was happening with his team, but he admitted it was a little stressful at times: "It's not an easy way to do it. It's tough on everybody, but it's great when you win." After losing the first game to the Kings, the Canadiens managed three straight overtime victories, bringing their amazing overtime win total to 10, before going on win the Cup in the final game.

186. C. 1932

Although the Toronto franchise had previously won the Stanley Cup both under the name of the Arenas and the St. Pats, the first Toronto Maple Leaf Stanley Cup win came in 1932. After slowly rebuilding the franchise when he acquired it in 1927, Conn Smythe finally put all the right ingredients together for the 1931–32 season. The Leafs were bolstered by their number one line (known as "The Kid Line") of Charlie Conacher, Joe Primeau and Busher Jackson, along with the goaltending of Lorne Chabot, the energy of King Clancy and the leadership of team captain Ace Bailey.

It was a tight race throughout the season, but the Leafs managed to finish second overall. After an easy quarterfinal win against the Chicago Blackhawks and an overtime win in the final game of the semifinals against the Montréal Maroons, the Leafs made it into the finals against the New York Rangers. In the best-of-five series, the Maple Leafs won the first game at Madison Square Garden in New York and took the second game in Boston (it was played there because the circus forced them out of New York). The Rangers were completely outclassed in the third game by the scoring of The Kid Line and the defensive leadership of Ace Bailey and King Clancy as Toronto easily swept the series in three straight.

187. D. Ottawa Senators

The San Jose Sharks were in their second year, and the Ottawa Senators were just getting their feet wet as a franchise during the 1992–93 NHL season when both finished with losing records. The Senators finished with an abysmal record of 10 wins, 70 losses and 4 ties, while the Sharks equaled their pathetic effort with 11 wins, 71 losses and 2 ties. No team has since come close to this dubious distinction.

188. **Which team holds the record for the longest undefeated streak at 35 games?**

A. Montréal Canadiens

B. Detroit Red Wings

C. Philadelphia Flyers

D. Boston Bruins

189. **In what year did the Stanley Cup cease to be a challenge Cup?**

A. 1909

B. 1910

C. 1915

D. 1926

190. **Which team did Bobby Orr end his amazing career with?**

A. Boston Bruins

B. Detroit Red Wings

C. Chicago Blackhawks

D. St. Louis Blues

191. **How many times have the Boston Bruins won the Stanley Cup?**

A. Two

B. Four

C. Five

D. Seven

188. C.   Philadelphia Flyers

The Philadelphia Flyers were just beginning to shake off the "Broad Street Bullies" image they had expertly cultivated during the '70s and were transitioning their team for the faster style that was being developed by the New York Islanders and the Edmonton Oilers. The Flyers, a team of aging veterans and young talent, were not expected to go very far when the 1979–80 season got underway. Head coach Pat Quinn was just entering into his first full year as coach of the team, having taken over halfway into the previous season. Pete Peeters had taken over in goal for the popular Bernie Parent and had yet to prove himself as a top level goaltender, but nonetheless, the Flyers started off the season with confidence. They won their season opener on October 14, 1979, against the Toronto Maple Leafs by a score of 4–3, and by mid-December they had yet to lose. By January 7, 1980, they had compiled an amazing record of 25 wins and 10 ties. That night, they played against the Minnesota North Stars and tried to extend their streak to 36 games but were defeated 7–2.

189. C. 1915

Up until 1915, professional teams from a number of leagues were allowed to declare a challenge against the reigning Stanley Cup champions. This meant that if the Ottawa Senators won the Cup in 1907, another team could immediately challenge them. By making it a challenge Cup, there could be several winners in one year. After 1915, Stanley Cup trustees decided that the Cup should be awarded in a playoff format, to be played by two teams that had won their regular season schedules. This allowed teams from the West, such as the Seattle Metropolitans of the Pacific Coast Hockey Association, to play for the Cup.

190. C. Chicago Blackhawks

After several injury-shortened seasons with the Boston Bruins, Bobby Orr decided to try his luck with the Chicago Blackhawks for the start of the 1976–77 season. He only played 20 games with the Hawks that season and another six games in the 1978–79 season before finally retiring because of serious knee problems.

191. C. Five

The Boston Bruins have won the Stanley Cup five times in Stanley Cup history. The Bruins won their first franchise Stanley Cup in 1929 with the help of goaltender Cecil "Tiny" Thompson and coach Art Ross. They won another Cup 10 years later with players Eddie Shore, Dit Clapper and goaltender Frank Brimsek. Their next Cup came in 1941 with goal scorers Bill Cowley and Milt Schmidt leading the way, and years later, Bobby Orr and Phil Esposito led the Bruins to two more Cups in 1970 and 1972.

192. **Which NHL team was the first to win three consecutive Stanley Cups?**

A.   Toronto Maple Leafs

B.   Montréal Canadiens

C.   Ottawa Senators

D.   Boston Bruins

193. **Which two teams hold the record for most shots in one game?**

A.   Detroit Red Wings versus Montréal Maroons

B.   Toronto Maple Leafs versus Boston Bruins

C.   New York Islanders versus Washington Capitals

D.   Philadelphia Flyers versus Pittsburgh Penguins

194. **Name one of the two teams to have had the most 50-goal scorers in the team's history.**

A.   Montréal Canadiens

B.   Pittsburgh Penguins

C.   Edmonton Oilers

D.   New York Islanders

192. A.   Toronto Maple Leafs

The Toronto Maple Leafs were the first NHL team to win three consecutive Stanley Cups. Their streak began in 1947 when they defeated the Montréal Canadiens and lasted until 1949 when they defeated the Detroit Red Wings.

193. B.   Toronto Maple Leafs versus Boston Bruins

The Toronto Maple Leafs and the Boston Bruins played the second-longest game in NHL history when they played through six extra overtime periods on April 3, 1933.

194. B.   Pittsburgh Penguins

The Pittsburgh Penguins have had seven 50-goal scorers since joining the NHL in 1967. They are Pierre Larouche (53 goals), Jean Pronovost (52), Rick Kehoe (55), Mike Bullard (51), Mario Lemieux (85), Kevin Stevens (54) and Jaromir Jagr (62). The Calgary Flames is the other team to also have seven players on the list: Lanny McDonald (66), Hakan Loob (50), Joe Nieuwendyk (51), Joe Mullen (51), Theoren Fleury (51), Gary Roberts (53) and Jarome Iginla (52).

Questions 195 – 197

195. **Which team was granted an NHL franchise to begin the 1999–2000 season?**

   A.   Nashville Predators

   B.   Atlanta Thrashers

   C.   Anaheim Mighty Ducks

   D.   Columbus Blue Jackets

196. **Name the first American-based team in the NHL.**

   A.   Detroit Cougars

   B.   Pittsburgh Pirates

   C.   Boston Bruins

   D.   New York Americans

197. **Which team holds the record for fewest shots in a single game?**

   A.   Toronto Maple Leafs

   B.   Cleveland Barons

   C.   Ottawa Senators

   D.   Detroit Red Wings

195. B.   Atlanta Thrashers

In the late 1990s and into the new millennium, the NHL expanded into the southern United States, but the only team to emerge during the 1999–2000 season was the Atlanta Thrashers.

196. C.   Boston Bruins

The Boston Bruins became the first American-based NHL team when they joined the league for the start of the 1924–25 NHL season. Despite having some talented players such as Jimmy Herberts and Alf Skinner, as well as the coaching of legend Art Ross, the Bruins finished their inaugural season with a pitiful record of six wins and 24 losses. The next season, the Pittsburgh Pirates and the New York Americans joined the NHL.

197. A.   Toronto Maple Leafs

On May 8, 2000, when the Toronto Maple Leafs met the New Jersey Devils, they had just six shots on goal in the entire game. The New Jersey Devils practiced to perfection the trap system that did not allow many shots on goal. The Leafs were frustrated the entire night and eventually lost the game 3–0. Right behind the Leafs are the 1978 Washington Capitals, which managed only seven shots against the Philadelphia Flyers on February 12, 1978, in a 4–1 loss.

198. Which team holds the modern-day record for the fewest losses in one season?

A. 1977–78 Montréal Canadiens

B. 1995–96 Detroit Red Wings

C. 1976–77 Montréal Canadiens

D. 1971–72 Boston Bruins

199. Which team holds the dubious record for being shutout the most times in one season?

A. Chicago Blackhawks

B. Toronto Maple Leafs

C. Ottawa Senators

D. New York Americans

200. How many Stanley Cup celebrations have there been in the city of Montréal?

A. 24

B. 26

C. 32

D. 41

198. C.   1976–77 Montréal Canadiens

The 1976–77 Montréal Canadiens were the best in NHL history. In 80 regular season games, the Habs won 60 games, lost only 8 and tied 12. With Ken Dryden in goal, Larry Robinson, Guy Lapointe and Serge Savard on defence, and forwards Bob Gainey, Guy Lafleur and Steve Shutt, the Canadiens were an unstoppable force.

199. A.   Chicago Blackhawks

During the same season when George Hainsworth of the Montréal Canadiens recorded 22 shutouts, the 1928–29 Chicago Blackhawks tallied a horrible record, being chur out a total of 20 times. They were so awful that they strung together eight consecutive games where they were shutout from February 7 to 28.

200. D.   41

The city of Montréal has been blessed with 41 Stanley Cup celebrations since the Lord Stanley's Mug was first awarded in 1893. As many people know, the Montréal Canadiens won the Cup 24 times, the Montréal Victorias five times, the Montréal Wanderers four times, the Montréal AAAs four times, the Montréal Shamrocks two times, and the Montréal Maroons took home the Cup two times.

Chapter Nine

The Weird and the Wacky

---

201. Who was the only player to have his toupee torn from his head during a professional hockey game?

A. Rick Green

B. Mats Sundin

C. Bobby Hull

D. Jacques Lemaire

202. When the Toronto Maple Leafs Red Kelly got to take the Stanley Cup for a day after the Leafs 1964 championship, what happened to the Cup that made him say, "That's why our family always laughs when we see players drinking champagne from the Cup"?

A. He got really drunk and threw up in the Cup.

B. His son played with the Cup when he had chicken pox.

C. His infant son did a "number one" and a "number two" in the Cup.

D. Someone used the Cup as a planter.

201. C. Bobby Hull

When Bobby Hull first broke into the league, he was known for two things: his offensive talent on the ice, and his golden locks of hair that flowed in the wind as he skated down the ice. With his chiseled good looks, the "Golden Jet" was the poster boy for the perfect NHL athlete, which made it all the more difficult for Hull when he started losing his hair. Unable to accept losing his hair, Hull became the first player in professional hockey history to wear a toupee during a professional game.

Of course, every other player knew Hull wore a hairpiece, because they could see it flying in the air as he skated down the ice, but no one was foolish enough to mess with the Golden Jet's new do. Hull had a pair of 38-centimetre biceps and was not one to shy away from a challenge. But one player in Hull's days in the World Hockey Association (WHA) had enough courage to take on Hull and find out for himself just what he was hiding underneath that rug. Curiosity finally overcame Steve Durbano, who played for the Birmingham Bulls of the WHA, on April 14, 1978, during a playoff game versus Bobby Hull's

Winnipeg Jets. At one point in the game, when Hull and Durbano were on the ice at the same time, a fight broke out in the corner of the rink. In the mix of bodies and arms, Durbano suddenly found that he had something soggy and wet in his hands, and when he looked down, he realized that he was holding Hull's toupee. Durbano immediately threw the rug to the ice, and everyone in the arena turned to see Hull's shining cranium exposed for all to gawk at. Too embarrassed to pick up his toupee or give Durbano a beating, Hull rushed off the ice into the dressing room and returned to action wearing a helmet on his head and several shades of red on his face.

**202. C.   His infant son did a "number one"
and a "number two" in the Cup.**

The most disgusting of all stories of strange things that have happened to the Stanley Cup occurred one day in 1964 when Red Kelly took the Cup to his home for the day. At the Kelly home, a photographer had been hired to take pictures of the family happily surrounding the Stanley Cup. After posing for a few photos, Kelly thought it would be a good idea to take a picture of his baby boy naked in the bowl of the Cup. The picture turned out to be a wonderful memory, but for the wrong reasons. When the photographer took the picture, and Kelly went to pick up his son, Kelly discovered that his little boy had left some memories of his own behind. "He did the whole load in the Cup," said Kelly. So from now on when you see players drinking from the Cup, you too will always have the image of a little baby's contribution to hockey history.

203. Name the only deaf player ever to play in the NHL.

A. Barry Gibbs

B. Bob Nevin

C. Mick Vukota

D. Jim Kyte

204. Who invented the saying "hat trick" for when a player scores three goals?

A. Detroit general manager Jack Adams

B. A Toronto hat maker

C. Montréal Canadiens head coach Toe Blake

D. NHL president Clarence Campbell

205. Who was the first NHL player to receive a lifetime suspension from hockey?

A. Marty McSorley

B. Earl Siebert

C. Billy Coutu

D. Eddie Shore

203. D.   Jim Kyte

In the history of the NHL, there have been many times when the athletes have done and accomplished amazing things, but no one had ever seen the likes of Jim Kyte when he joined the league in 1983 as the only deaf hockey player to play for an NHL team. At 6 foot 5, 210 pounds, Kyte was the perfect stay-at-home defenceman, able to clear out any opponent in front of his goaltender's crease. Although being considered legally deaf did limit his performance on the ice at the time, it didn't create any serious problems. Unable to hear the whistle on an offside or icing call, on the odd occasion Kyte often continued battling in the corners with a confused opponent. He wore a hearing aid to help boost what little hearing he had, but in the noise of the arena, Kyte had to rely on his other senses to get by. After spending several years with the Winnipeg Jets, he bounced around several other teams in the league before settling with the San Jose Sharks, which was where he retired from the game after 13 successful years in the NHL.

204. B.   A Toronto hat maker

The long-standing hockey tradition of throwing hats onto the ice after a player scores three goals hasn't always been part of the game. Before 1946, scoring three goals was called just that, three goals, and not a "hat trick" as it is more commonly known today. The term came about in 1946, when Chicago Blackhawks forward Alex Kaleta walked into a hat shop in Toronto owned by Sammy Taft. Kaleta bet the hatter that if he scored three goals in the game that night against the Maple Leafs, Taft would have to give him a hat of his choice for free. Knowing that scoring three goals was quite unlikely, Taft took Kaleta's bet. That night, Kaleta scored three goals and then walked into Taft's hat store the next day to collect his winnings.

The newspapers got wind of the story and quoted Taft saying, "Yeah, that was some *trick* he pulled to get that *hat*." From that day on, the feat became known simply as a "hat trick." Ever the smart businessman, Taft used the publicity to help promote his store. Every time a Toronto player scored three goals, he gave him a free hat. The term stuck, and now the crowd supplies the hats for the players by throwing them on the ice after a hat trick.

205. C.   Billy Coutu

Billy Coutu was one of the fiercest competitors in the early years of the game. His intensity on the ice was what made him a good defenceman, but it also got him into a lot of trouble. Coutu played for the Hamilton Tigers and the Montréal Canadiens before being traded to the Boston Bruins at the start of the 1926 regular season. He began his career with the Bruins on a bad note when in his first practice with the team he took offense to some good-natured ribbing from team-mate Eddie Shore and body slammed him on the ice, severing part of Shore's ear in the process.

Billy Coutu continued with his violent ways into the 1927 Stanley Cup playoffs. In game four of the finals between the Bruins and the Ottawa Senators, he started a bench-clearing brawl. However, before making a judgement, you should be aware that the fight was at the request of head coach Art Ross. During the altercation, Coutu ended up punching referee Jerry Laflamme and was suspended from the NHL for life, becoming the first-ever player to receive the dishonour—but not the last.

206. Who was the last player to score a goal in the 20th century?

A. Mats Sundin

B. Marian Hossa

C. Valerie Bure

D. Brett Hull

207. In 1987, what felony did Dino Ciccarelli plead guilty to?

A. Robbery

B. Drunk driving

C. Drug possession

D. Indecent exposure

208. Which team did not receive the Stanley Cup after winning it?

A. Boston Bruins in 1929

B. Montréal Canadiens in 1930

C. Detroit Red Wings in 1936

D. Toronto Maple Leafs in 1947

206. D.   Brett Hull

Brett Hull scored his 601st career goal in his 900th game at 9:30 PM central time in Dallas, Texas, making him the last person to score a goal in the NHL in the 20th century.

207. D.   Indecent exposure

Dino Ciccarelli liked the feeling of walking around in his house in the nude or sometimes seminude. The only problem was that one day when he went outside to retrieve the morning newspaper, he forgot to slip on a pair of pants and ended up giving the neighbours a little more than they bargained for. A neighbour called the police, and Ciccarelli got charged with indecent exposure. He pled guilty and was forced to serve 50 hours of community service.

208. D.   Toronto Maple Leafs in 1947

Playing the Montréal Canadiens in the finals in 1947, the Toronto Maple Leafs were ahead in the series three games to two, but the Cup was not brought to Toronto for game six. Leafs general manager Conn Smythe had left the Cup behind in Montréal because he did not want his players to get overconfident at the sight of the Cup. The plan worked to perfection, but when the Leafs won the final game, they had no Cup to celebrate with or to drink from.

209. Name the only goaltender to win the Hart Trophy as the league's MVP while playing for a last-place team.

A. Jose Theodore

B. Al Rollins

C. Dave Kerr

D. Chuck Rayner

210. When a team wins the Stanley Cup, each player gets a day with the Cup. Who was the first player to take the Cup to Europe?

A. Peter Forsberg

B. Bobby Holik

C. Mats Naslund

D. Anders Kallur

211. Which song does the NHL forbid from being played at games?

A. Bob Marley's "I Shot the Sheriff"

B. The children's song, "Three Blind Mice"

C. Chuck Berry's " My Ding-A-Ling"

D. James Brown's "I'm Black and I'm Proud"

209. B.   Al Rollins

When the NHL awards are handed out at the end of the season, sometimes they are given to players who might not be on the Stanley Cup–winning team or have won the scoring championship but have made a significant impact on the team. The Hart Trophy is tailor-made for an individual effort that makes the team much stronger. When goaltender Al Rollins of the 1954 Chicago Blackhawks was chosen as the recipient of the Hart Trophy as the league's most valuable player, the hockey world was caught a little off guard. That a goaltender with 12 wins and 47 losses could be chosen as MVP was surprising. But on close inspection, Rollins deserved every bit of credit for standing between the Hawks pipes that season. The 1953–54 season was a pitiful one for the Chicago Blackhawks. Every single game was a struggle, and night after night poor Rollins had to face more than his share of rubber. He had let in 213 goals and recorded a goals-against-average of 3.23.

Of course, with such stats, Rollins was over-looked when it came time for the All-Star game. But when voting time came around for the Hart Trophy selection, the voters thought that Rollins deserved a nod for his Herculean efforts in goal. It's not that Rollins was a terrible goalie, on the contrary, he was excellent. It just happened to be the year the Chicago Blackhawks were the worst team the league had seen in years. Voters knew that if Rollins had not been in goal, the Black-hawks might not have won the 12 games they actually did win.

210. A.   Peter Forsberg

Although European hockey players have been in the league for decades, the first player to take the Stanley Cup on a trans-Atlantic flight was Peter Forsberg in 1996 when his Colorado Ava-lanche won the Cup. He took the Cup to his hometown of Ornskoldsvik in northern Sweden.

211. B. The children's song, "Three Blind Mice"

In the old days, organists were responsible for keeping the crowd excited and into the game. Today, DJs just pop in CDs or plug in the latest MP3 selected from a huge library of music, but one song is still not allowed to be played in any arena. It is the timeless children's tune about the terror that three visually impaired rodents inflict on an unsuspecting farmer's wife, who promptly turns around and chops off their tails with a carving knife. The reason for the song being banned is simple. Before the league added a second referee on the ice, only two linesmen and one referee patrolled the ice—three officials. It is not uncommon for players and fans to yell out the phrase, "What are you, Ref, blind?" Therefore, in the league's infinite wisdom, they considered playing the song "Three Blind Mice" as a way of provoking anger toward the officials, who are by league rule, above criticism by players and coaches.

212. Who said "Just charge me with the usual"?

A.   Craig MacTavish

B.   Marty McSorley

C.   Bob Probert

D.   Terry Sawchuk

213. What memorable fashion faux pas did the Philadelphia Flyers and the Hartford Whalers commit during the 1982–83 season?

A.   They changed their jersey colour to a bright neon orange.

B.   Wings were printed on the backs of their jersey.

C.   The entire team wore white skates.

D.   They replaced the half pants with full-length pants.

214. Which was the last Stanley Cup–winning team to boast an all-Canadian line-up?

A.   The 1993 Montréal Canadiens

B.   The 1975 Philadelphia Flyers

C.   The 1955 Detroit Red Wings

D.   The 1960 Montréal Canadiens

212. C. Bob Probert

Throughout his career, Bob Probert was no stranger to controversy—nor to trouble. The Windsor, Ontario native who broke into the league with the Detroit Red Wings in 1985–86 was arrested twice in the span of eight months for driving under the influence of alcohol. He was fined thousands of dollars and had his driver's licence revoked. Probert's problems with alcohol foreshadowed things to come, as he continued to deteriorate, graduating from booze to cocaine. On March 2, 1989, he was again arrested, this time by U.S. border agents after a package of cocaine, valued at $1500, fell out of his shorts during a strip search. The response from the NHL was swift and fierce. He was banished from the NHL for life, becoming only the fourth player in the history of the league to receive such a dubious honour.

After serving his time in a U.S. jail, Probert was reinstated on March 2, 1990, by the NHL, which had decided to soften its stance. In July 1994, he was involved in a motorcycle accident in which he sustained serious injuries. When police arrived on the scene and found the injured Probert, he simply said to them, "Just charge me with the usual." Probert's alcohol level was three times the legal limit at the time of the crash, and trace amounts of cocaine were found in his system. He continued his bad boy routine even after his retirement from hockey in 2002, when he was involved in a street fight and had to be tasered by police.

213. D.   They replaced the half pants with full-length pants.

Looking back to the 1980s, many of us would shake our heads at some of the awful fashion mistakes we made. The NHL was not immune to such errors of judgement either, which was made clear on opening day of the Philadelphia Flyers' and Hartford Whalers' season. Although most hockey teams had made it through the polyester and glitter of the '70s, the '80s claimed its first fashion victims when the Flyers and the Whalers hit the ice wearing one-piece pants called "Cooperalls." Rather than sticking with the traditional short pants and hockey socks that had been used since the dawn of professional hockey, the Whalers and Flyers management, in their infinite wisdom, thought that ankle-length pants that slipped over a player's protective girdle and kneepads would look far better. They were wrong! The Whalers took the brunt of the jokes, with their garish green monochrome pants and sweaters eliciting many snickers from players and fans alike. The experiment was brief, lasting only one season. After the Cooperalls debacle, the league outlawed long pants league-wide. Fans and players could not say thank you enough.

214. B.   The 1975 Philadelphia Flyers

The 1975 Philadelphia Flyers were the last team to win the Stanley Cup with an all-Canadian line-up. The 1993 Montréal Canadiens were the last team to win the Cup with an all-North-American line-up.

215. **Who was touted as the "female Wayne Gretzky"?**

A. Cammi Granato

B. Hayley Wickenheiser

C. Stacy Wilson

D. Cassie Campbell

216. **Which NHL coach played one game as a goaltender after the regular net-minder was injured?**

A. Lester Patrick

B. Jack Adams

C. Art Ross

D. Newsy Lalonde

217. **Why was game two of the 1951 playoffs between the Toronto Maple Leafs and the Boston Bruins cancelled?**

A. Because of a curfew

B. The lights went out

C. All the players had the flu

D. Players strike

215. B. Hayley Wickenheiser

In a CBC TV interview in 1994, 15-year-old Hayley Wickenheiser talked about her talents as a hockey player—the "female Wayne Gretzky" comparisons and the possibility of one day maybe playing in a men's professional league. "I guess I would want to do that, but I don't know if it would be realistic. The size and strength differences are so incredible that it's pretty tough to do." Years later, she would have surprised her 15-year-old self at how far she had come. She climbed to the top of women's professional hockey with five World Championship titles and has just added Olympic gold to her collection as well.

At the end of 2002, she travelled to Europe, where she quickly found a spot in a professional men's league in Finland with the Kirkkonummi Salamat club. She surpassed a barrier no woman had ever accomplished when she scored her first goal in January 2003. Wickenheiser has brought much needed attention to women's hockey, opening up the game to a whole new generation of female players who never would have dreamed of playing hockey if it had not been for women such as herself.

216. A. Lester Patrick

Like a scene out of a Hollywood movie, 44-year-old New York Rangers head coach and manager Lester Patrick put on a pair of goalie pads and led his team to victory in a Stanley Cup finals game, securing a definite spot in the annals of hockey history. It happened in the 1928 Stanley Cup finals when Patrick's New York Rangers took on the Montréal Maroons in game two of a best-of-five series. The regular goaltender, Lorne Chabot, was taken out of the game because of a serious eye injury. In the early days of hockey, teams did not have backup goaltenders as they do today, so if a goaltender sustained a serious injury, an emergency stand-in had to be found quickly or the team had to forfeit the game. Desperate to find a replacement, Patrick asked the Maroons bench boss if Chabot could be replaced by the Ottawa Senators goaltender Alex Connel, who just happened to be at the game that night. The Maroons quickly turned down their request, saying it was against league rules, but they did offer up a solution of their own. "Why not put Lester in the net if you need a goaltender that bad?" said Maroons head coach Eddie Gerrard. What they didn't count on was Lester Patrick's sense of pride. He responded with, "I will, by God. I will!"

Patrick had donned goalie pads on a few occasions, but never in such a high-pressure situation as the Stanley Cup finals. Quickly dressing himself in Chabot's gear, Patrick hit the ice, stretched his legs and readied himself for the attack. He performed remarkably well. The Maroons peppered the grey-haired goaltender with shot after shot, but Patrick held the fort. Crouching low to the ice, he stopped all but one shot that beat him in the third period, tying the game and sending it into overtime. During overtime, the stand-in goalie defended his goal like a seasoned professional. To Patrick's relief, the Rangers finally won the game with a goal by Frank Boucher. Patrick was hoisted atop his players' shoulders after the game and paraded around the arena like a conquering hero. Inspired by their coach's effort, the Rangers went on to defeat the Montréal Maroons and brought the Stanley Cup back to the United States for the second time in the team's history.

217. A. Because of a curfew

The second game had to be cancelled after one overtime period because of a curfew in Toronto. The game was replayed the next day, and the Leafs won by a score of 3–0.

218. **Name the famous player who scored the game-winning goal for the Toronto Maple Leafs in the 1951 Stanley Cup playoffs.**

A. Gus Mortson

B. Ted Kennedy

C. Howie Meeker

D. Bill Barilko

219. **Who were the first two goalies to fight in the Stanley Cup playoffs?**

A. Patrick Roy and Mike Vernon

B. Turk Broda and Harry Lumley

C. Terry Sawchuk and Jim Henry

D. Patrick Roy and Chris Osgood

220. **What position in the draft was Dominik Hasek chosen overall?**

A. 12th overall

B. 55th overall

C. 190th overall

D. 207th overall

218. D. Bill Barilko

In the history of the game, a lot of heroes have emerged, but none were elevated to hero status faster than a young Toronto Maple Leaf defenceman named Bill Barilko. After only five seasons in the NHL, Barilko was considered a solid stay-at-home defenceman known more for his thundering body checks than for his goal-scoring ability. But it was one goal in particular that he would forever be remembered. The Maple Leafs were up three games to one on the Montréal Canadiens in the Stanley Cup finals. The series could have gone either way as each game went into overtime, but it was the Leafs that came out on the right side with heroics from stars such as Ted Kennedy and Sid Smith. Game five was no different from the previous four games, remaining close through each period. The Canadiens were leading 2–1 with just a few minutes left in the last period. Leafs head coach Joe Primeau pulled goaltender Al Rollins and prayed for the miracle that his team could score and send the game into yet another overtime. He got his wish when Tod Sloan fought his way to the front of the Montréal goal and picked up a rebound from Canadiens netminder Gerry McNeil. The Leafs tied the game and kept alive the hopes of taking home the Cup that night. Primeau was always nervous in sudden-death overtime, so he instructed his team to play it safe on the defence.

The Canadiens had speedy players such as Maurice Richard and Bernie Geoffrion, who could break free and score given the smallest window of opportunity. But luckily, one Leafs defenceman did not take the instructions well. Two minutes had passed when the Leafs broke into the Canadiens zone and set up a perimeter around the Montréal net. When a shot bounced off McNeil, Barilko seized his chance, darted in from the blue line and flipped the puck over the prostrate Montréal goaltender. At 2:53 of the extra time, Barilko won the Leafs the Cup. That summer Barilko was a Toronto hero. Unfortunately, this was his last brush with glory. To end the summer, Barilko and his buddy Henry Hudson decided to get a little relaxation by flying up north to spend the weekend fishing. Sometime during their flight, something went wrong, and they never made it to their destination. Leafs owner Conn Smythe offered a $10,000 reward for anyone who had information leading to the whereabouts of Barilko, but no one seemed to know what had happened to the young defenceman.

As time passed, rumours were bandied about that Barilko was teaching hockey to the communists or was smuggling gold in northern Ontario.

Eventually the exhaustive search was called off. The mystery of his disappearance was solved 11 years later, in 1962, when a provincial forestry department pilot spotted a shining piece of metal near Cochrane, Ontario. When authorities travelled on foot to the area, they found Barilko's plane, with two skeletons still strapped in their seats. From then on, the legend of the young Leafs defenceman only grew larger, and it eventually hit popular culture when the rock group The Tragically Hip penned "Fifty Mission Cap," a song written about Barilko.

219. B.   Turk Broda and Harry Lumley

The first confirmed battle royale between two netminders happened during game two of the Detroit Red Wings and the Toronto Maple Leafs Stanley Cup finals series. There was no declared winner of the tilt, but Lumley did have the size advantage over the lighter and shorter Broda.

220. D.   207th overall

Dominik Hasek was selected 207th overall by the Chicago Blackhawks in the 1983 NHL Entry Draft. Hasek has gone on to have an outstanding career, earning gold at the 1998 Olympics, countless individual awards and a Stanley Cup in 2002 with the Detroit Red Wings.

221. Who was the first black player in the NHL?

A.   Grant Fuhr

B.   Willie O'Ree

C.   Pokey Reddick

D.   Tony McKegney

222. What is the most common retired number in the NHL?

A.   1

B.   7

C.   9

D.   10

223. What was different about the 2005 NHL Entry Draft?

A.   The order was selected by lottery.

B.   There was no clear number one pick.

C.   The Detroit Red Wings did not have a selection.

D.   No Europeans were chosen in the first round.

221. B.   Willie O'Ree

A young Toronto-born hockey player by the name of Herb Carnegie, who played in the Québec Senior Hockey League for the Québec Aces in the early 1940s, was widely recognized as one of the best players in the league, but because he was black, he was denied a chance at playing in the NHL. Toronto Maple Leafs owner Conn Smythe even told the young player, "Herb, I'd sign you in a minute if I could turn you white."

The first player to actually get his chance in the big league was Willie O'Ree, over a decade later, when the Boston Bruins called him up from the minors to play two games against the Montréal Canadiens starting on January 18, 1958. O'Ree did not score during his brief stay with the Bruins, but he changed the game forever. Like Jackie Robinson had done 10 years earlier in Major League Baseball, O'Ree broke the NHL's colour barrier. However, it still wasn't easy to be black in the NHL. O'Ree was called up to the Bruins again three years later for the last half of the 1960–61 season. This time he went with the team as it travelled to other cities, and the team accepted him like it would any other player. However, during these away games, racial slurs were thrown at him from fans and opposing players on a nightly basis. "They were mean to me in places like Detroit and New York. But never in Boston," said O'Ree in Brian McFarlane's book *Best of the Original Six*. "I'll never forget how my teammates there—men like Johnny Bucyk, Doug Mohns, Charlie Burns and Don McKenney—took care of me. They accepted me totally. All of them had class." When asked about the Bruins new player, head coach Milt Schmidt said, "He isn't black. He's a Bruin."

But one night the taunting from opposing players and fans got out of hand after an incident involving O'Ree and the Chicago Blackhawks forward Eric Nesterenko. Trouble started when Nesterenko went into the corner to check O'Ree off the puck, and the butt-end of his stick went right into O'Ree's mouth and knocked out two teeth. When O'Ree retaliated by swinging his stick at Nesterenko's head, the crowd got out of hand, hurling racial slurs down on O'Ree. Both players were thrown out of the game, but O'Ree had trouble getting off the ice because fans were throwing anything they could get their hands on at him. O'Ree required a police escort just to get him off the ice and out of the arena. The game was stopped to prevent further violence. O'Ree only played 45 games with the Boston Bruins before being traded to the Montréal Canadiens organization, where he spent the rest of his career in the minor system. By crossing the colour line, O'Ree paved the way for kids who might never have got the chance to the play in the NHL had it not been for him.

222. B.   7

The number 7 has been worn by some of the greatest players in the game. The first to have his number 7 retired was the Montréal Canadiens Howie Morenz in 1937, after his death. Other notable retired number 7s are Bill Barber of the Philadelphia Flyers, Paul Coffey of the Edmonton Oilers, Phil Esposito of the Boston Bruins, Rod Gilbert of the New York Rangers, Yvon Labre of the Washington Capitals, Ted Lindsay of the Detroit Red Wings, Rick Martin of the Buffalo Sabres and Neal Broten of the Dallas Stars.

223. A.   The order was selected by lottery.

Because the previous season had been cancelled as a result of the NHL lockout, the league was unable to determine in the regular fashion the order of selection for the draft, which is usually based on the team's position at the end of the season. So for the 2005 draft, the order was selected by lottery, with the Pittsburgh Penguins winning the number one spot and selecting Sidney Crosby as their number one pick overall.

Questions 224 – 225

224. **When Team Canada won Olympic gold in 2002, how many years had it been since the last time they won gold?**

A. 8 years

B. 24 years

C. 32 years

D. 50 years

225. **Name the only player to score twice on the same penalty shot.**

A. Eric Desjardins

B. Dickie Moore

C. Andy Bathgate

D. Jack Hamilton

224. D.   50 years

When hockey was still in its infancy, Canada was the uncontested ruler of the hockey world. Nothing better illustrates Canada's global dominance of the game than the success its team had in the first Winter Olympic Games in 1924 in Chamonix, France. The Toronto Granites were selected to represent Canada on the international stage, and they completely dominated the Olympics. Led by Reginald "Hooley" Smith and Harry "Moose" Watson, the Canadians faced an unprepared Czechoslovakian team. The Czechs could barely control the puck while the Canadians ran circles around them. When the smoke cleared, the Canadians had potted 30 goals, and the Czechs could not even get one. Canada then beat the Swedish team 20–0, the Swiss 33–0 and ultimately claiming gold against the United States by a score of 6–0. They won a string of gold medals only broken up in 1936 by the British hockey team who won the gold (the British team was made up of Canadians). Their last gold medal at the Olympics came in 1952 at the Oslo Winter Games.

It would take 50 years before Canada could once again hold its head high on the international stage. Doubters, deniers and disbelievers were ready to watch the Canadians miss their chance at gold during the 2002 Salt Lake City Winter Games, but the team knew this was one of their best chances. Led by captain Mario Lemieux, the Canadian squad included Joe Sakic, Jarome Iginla, Paul Kariya, Steve Yzerman, Theoren Fleury and goaltender Martin Brodeur, to name just a few. The Canadians were recognized as one of the top teams but were dogged by history. Canada surprised their doubters and made it into the gold medal game 50 years to the day that they last won. They were set to play a strong American team with the great goaltending of Mike Richter.

Although the U.S. was the first to score, it seemed to make the Canadians more determined. The highlight goal of the game came when Mario Lemieux, Chris Pronger and Paul Kariya broke into the U.S. zone. The Mario Lemieux of the 1980s came back for a brief moment of magic when he avoided the Pronger pass by letting it glide between his legs, faking out the defenceman and the goaltender who had prepared for the Lemieux shot. Instead, Lemieux had let it go to Paul Kariya, who scored with an easy snapshot into the open cage. From then on, it was Canada's game. The game ended with a score of 5–2, and Canada once again was at the top of the hockey world after a 50-year absence.

225. D.   Jack Hamilton

Jack Hamilton of the 1944 Toronto Maple Leafs accomplished something no other player ever will again. He scored twice on one penalty shot. During a game between the Boston Bruins and the Toronto Maple Leafs, Jack Hamilton was awarded a penalty shot after being hauled down by Dit Clapper in front of the Bruins net. Referee Norm Lamport made an error, which no one noticed, and placed the puck at centre ice. Hamilton took the puck, skated in and put the puck past goaltender Bert Gardiner.

Once the Boston bench realized what had just happened, they protested that the shot be retaken because the referee had placed the puck on the wrong line. The referee acknowledged his error, placed the puck on the Bruins blueline and ordered Hamilton to retake the shot. Hamilton skated back in on Gardiner and shot another puck past him for a goal, making him the only player to score twice on the same penalty shot. The goal was also his first hat trick in the league.

Chapter Ten

Experts' Corner

---

226. Name the first European player to win the Art Ross Trophy.

Answer: As Wayne Gretzky and Mario Lemieux reached the later stages of their careers, they no longer held their vice-like grip on the top scoring spot in the league, leaving an opportunity for a brash young Czech forward with a bad haircut named Jaromir Jagr to take over the scoring summit. He scored 70 points in the lockout-shortened season in 1994–95 to win the title.

227. What player was signed to the longest professional hockey contract in history?

Answer: On January 26, 1979, the day of Wayne Gretzky's 18th birthday, he was signed to a 20-year personal services contract by Peter Pocklington, owner of the then World Hockey Association (WHA) Edmonton Oilers.

**228. What notable job did Clarence Camp-
bell have before becoming president of
the NHL?**

Answer: When World War II broke out, Clarence Campbell immediately enlisted in the
Canadian Armed Forces. After the war, his back-
ground in law helped him get a position on the
Queen's Counsel, and he helped prosecute several high-profile Nazi commanders for crimes
against humanity.

**229. Why did Maurice Richard choose the
number 9 as his jersey number?**

Answer: When Maurice Richard first joined
the Montréal Canadiens, he was randomly given
jersey number 15, but after the birth of his first
daughter, he decided he needed a change. Richard chose the number 9, after how much his
daughter weighed at birth. It is hard to imagine
Richard wearing any other number.

230. What team won the most playoff series in a row?

Answer: The Montréal Canadiens of the 1950s and their five Stanley Cups in a row might be a top choice, but the playoffs back then only consisted of a total of three series before a Stanley Cup winner was decided. The correct answer is the New York Islanders dynasty of the 1980s. During their reign as Stanley Cup champions, the Islanders won 16 straight playoff series and added another three in 1984, the year the Oilers beat them in the finals to end their streak at 19 straight games.

231. What where the two names of the Toronto NHL franchise before they became the Toronto Maple Leafs?

Answer: In the first three years of the NHL, the franchise was known as the Toronto Arenas, and in 1919 they changed their name to the Toronto St. Patricks. (To get even more bonus points, you will also know that they were sometimes referred to as the Toronto Blueshirts.)

232. What American-based hockey team was the first to win the Stanley Cup?

Answer: Just before the formation of the NHL, a team from Seattle called the Metropolitans surprised the hockey world in 1917 and won the Stanley Cup, thereby becoming the first American-based hockey team to win the Cup. The Pacific Coast Hockey Association team beat the Montréal Canadiens three games to one, easily taking the championship. Nationalistic Canadian hockey fans need not worry, however, as the first U.S. hockey team to win the Cup was mostly made up of Canadian players.

233. Who is the youngest player to be named as team captain?

Answer: Sidney Crosby of the Pittsburgh Penguins became the youngest player to wear the captain's "C" on his jersey at the tender age of 19 years and 297 days. The previous record holder was Vincent Lecavalier of the Tampa Bay Lightning, at 19 years and 324 days.

234. Why did Ed Belfour change his jersey number from 30 to 20 when he was with the Chicago Blackhawks?

Answer: Ed Belfour began his career wearing the number 30, but after spending one season with the Blackhawks goaltending coach Vladislav Tretiak, he changed his number to 20 in honour of Tretiak.

235. What was the only number never to have been worn in the NHL?

Answer: When the Montréal Canadiens Guillaume Latendresse broke into the NHL on September 29, 2006, he became the first person in league history ever to wear the number 84.

236. Why does Sidney Crosby wear the number 87?

Answer: Sidney Crosby wears the number 87 because he was born in 1987.

237. Who was the last Montréal Canadiens player to score 50 goals?

Answer: The Montréal Canadiens have been without a 50-goal scorer since Stephane Richer scored 51 goals during the 1989–90 regular season.

238. Who did the Toronto Maple Leafs select with their one and only first overall NHL Entry Draft selection?

Answer: The Toronto Maple Leafs used their one and only number one pick in the 1985 draft to select Wendel Clark from Saskatoon.

239. Sidney Crosby's father, Troy Crosby, was selected in the NHL Entry Draft in what year and by which team?

Answer: Troy Crosby was selected 240th overall in 1984 by the Montréal Canadiens. He never played a single game in the NHL.

240. Who is the only person to have his name inscribed on the Stanley Cup as player, general manager and head coach?

Answer: The legendary Jack Adams wore almost every hat possible in professional hockey. After a brilliant amateur career, he turned pro in 1917 and signed up with the eventual Stanley Cup–winning Toronto Arenas. After spending a few years in the Pacific Coast Hockey League, he rejoined the NHL with the Toronto St. Pats for the 1925–26 season before moving to another Stanley Cup–winning team in 1927 with the Ottawa Senators. Immediately after retiring, Adams was lured back into hockey by NHL president Frank Calder and became the head coach and general manager of the new Detroit Cougars franchise. It wasn't until 1936 that Adams finally won another Cup with the now Detroit Red Wings, for which his name was engraved on the Cup once again, but this time as coach and manager, and then again as just manager in 1943, 1950, 1952, 1954 and the last one in 1955.

241. Who is the only player to score his 500th career goal as a hat trick?

Answer: Mats Sundin of the Toronto Maple Leafs scored his 500th career goal on October 14, 2006. The goal was the game winner in overtime, a hat trick and his 500th of his career. Now that's doing it in style!

242. Who is the only retired NHL player to win the scoring title yet is not in the Hall of Fame?

Answer: Despite recording 82 points and winning the scoring race in 1943–44, Herb Cain has yet to be inducted into the Hockey Hall of Fame. However, it is not surprising that Cain remains outside the Hall—his scoring record was achieved during the war years when it seemed widely understood that underachievers populated the league, because all the good players were off fighting in Europe. In 570 career games, Cain scored 206 goals and 194 assists, making him an unlikely candidate to ever make the Hall of Fame.

243. Name all four franchises to play in only one season in the NHL.

Answer:

(1) The Montréal Wanderers might have been a team to reckon with in the NHL, but a fire that destroyed their arena midway through the first NHL season in 1917 ruined any hopes for the franchise's future in the league.

(2) The Philadelphia Quakers spent one season in the NHL in 1930–31 and failed to impress anyone in the city of Brotherly Love to warrant keeping the franchise with a dismal record of 4-36-4.

(3) The Québec Bulldogs, which, despite the presence of superstar Joe Malone and his 39 goals in 24 games, could only manage four wins the entire season. After that dismal season, any future investment in the old city would have to wait several decades.

(4) The St. Louis Eagles, which had just one season to prove that the southern United States was not yet ready for hockey. At the end of the 1934–35 season, the Eagles had a record of 11 wins, 31 losses and 6 ties.

244. Who was the first goaltender to register an assist in an NHL game?

Answer: Montréal Canadiens goaltending legend Georges Vezina became the first NHL goalie to earn an assist when the team beat the Toronto Arenas by a score of 6–3 on December 28, 1918.

245. Who wrote the *Hockey Night in Canada* theme song?

Answer: Every Saturday night, Canadians from coast to coast gather in front of their TVs for the weekly *Hockey Night in Canada* broadcast to watch their favourite teams do battle. However, the ritual is not complete without the familiar "Danda-da-dan-da-Danda-da-dan-daaa…" Vancouver-born composer Dolores Claman wrote Canada's unofficial national anthem in 1968. She wrote the theme song with the idea of copying a TV adventure show or a gladiator movie.

246. **Name the only member of the Boston Bruins to score at least 500 goals while wearing a Bruins jersey.**

Answer: You might think it was Phil Esposito or maybe Bobby Orr, but the only member of the Boston Bruins to score more than 500 goals in a Bruins jersey was the great Johnny Bucyk. Although he got his start with the Detroit Red Wings in 1955, he played just two seasons with the club, scoring 11 goals. The remainder of his illustrious career was spent in Beantown, where he racked up 545 goals for the Bruins until his retirement in 1978.

247. **Who was the first hockey player to die in a plane crash?**

Answer: Hobey Baker never played a single game in the NHL, but he is still considered one of the greatest players to ever put on a pair of skates. He was the first true American-born hockey star who thrilled fans with his flamboyant style and blistering speed. He was the kind of man who inspired other men and drove the hearts of women wild, so much so that F. Scott Fitzgerald wrote his character into his book *This Side of Paradise*. Baker was held up as the symbol of an innocent generation who grew up quickly during the outbreak of World War I. His hockey career was short, but it was filled with great moments. When hockey legend Lester Patrick once saw him play, he immediately offered Baker $3500 to turn pro in Canada, but Baker refused, preferring to play hockey simply for the love of the game.

When the war broke out, Baker left behind the game he loved to fight for the country he loved. He joined the air force and fought the same way he played hockey, with passion and reckless abandon. But that recklessness eventually caught up with him. Miraculously, Baker survived his tour of duty, and a few days before he was set to return to the U.S. he wanted to take one last flight. He took a recently repaired plane up in the air and had just leveled off close to the base when the plane's engine suddenly cut off. Baker tried everything he could do to land the plane safely, but he died in the resulting crash. He was just 26 years old.

248. What senior pro team did Jean Beliveau play for before joining the Montréal Canadiens?

Answer: In the early '50s, everyone in Québec City knew the name of Jean Beliveau. He was the star player with the junior Québec Citadels and then became a bigger star when he joined the senior pro Québec Aces. His good looks and approachable manner made him the number one celebrity in the city. When the Montréal Canadiens wanted to sign him, he refused at first, saying that he was comfortable with his life in Québec City. And when the Canadiens offered him a juicy contract as large as the one Maurice Richard was getting, Beliveau declined again because he was already a star in Québec and was making even more money than Richard. To get Beliveau out of Québec City and into a Montréal Canadiens jersey, the club's owner, Senator Donat Raymond, had to buy the entire Québec Senior Hockey League, only then did Beliveau finally sign with the Canadiens in 1953.

249. Why was Ted Lindsay traded to the Chicago Blackhawks in 1957?

Answer: On July 24, 1957, Detroit Red Wings manager Jack Adams got rid of a horn in his side. The problem all started in 1952 when Ted Lindsay was appointed to the board of the NHL's Pension Society and became a vocal opponent to the owners' refusal to let the players view the accounting books of their pension. By 1956, Lindsay had become so frustrated with the lack of progress and railroading from the owners that he approached a fellow player, Doug Harvey of the Montréal Canadiens, about forming a players' union or association. By February 12, 1957, when Lindsay and Harvey decided to announce the new players' union, every player in the league had signed up. Jack Adams had enough of Lindsay's muckraking and traded him to the basement dwelling Chicago Blackhawks, along with Glenn Hall, as punishment. Lindsay's hope for a players' association was crushed when Gordie Howe and Red Kelly resigned from the legal battle and soon after the association died.

250. What is the Bud Light Trophy awarded for?

Answer: The Bud Light Trophy is awarded to the player with the best plus/minus rating during the year. It was first awarded in 1998 to the St. Louis Blues Chris Pronger who had a rating of +47.

Ten Bonus Questions

251. Name the goaltender who almost lost his life during a game when someone sliced his neck open with a skate.

Answer: Buffalo Sabres goaltender Clint Malarchuk almost lost his life on March 22, 1989, when St. Louis Blues forward Steve Tuttle collided with a Sabres defenceman and was sent flying through the air at Malarchuk. In the collision, Tuttle's skate sliced into Malarchuk's neck, severing his jugular vein. Were it not for the quick thinking of trainer Jim Pizzutelli, who slowed the loss of blood until doctors could operate, Malarchuk would have died that night.

252. Who was the first rookie to score 100 points?

Answer: Peter Stastny was 24 years old when he joined the Québec Nordiques for the 1980–81 season. The Czechoslovakian native scored 39 goals and 70 assists on his way to a 109-point season. Wayne Gretzky was not eligible as a rookie when he scored 137 points in his first year in the league.

253. Who coached the most games in NHL history?

Answer: The coach with the most games, most wins and most Stanley Cups to his name is none other than the great Scotty Bowman. From 1967 to 2002, Bowman coached 2141 games, winning 1244 and losing only 584. He began his career with the St. Louis Blues, then spent some of his most successful years with the Montréal Canadiens, then the Buffalo Sabres, Pittsburgh Penguins, and finally with the Detroit Red Wings.

254. What was special about the game between the Los Angeles Kings and the Minnesota North Stars on November 10, 1979?

Answer: At every NHL game, a bucket of pucks is on standby for the referees and linesmen to use in case one goes flying into the crowd or splits apart after hitting the goalpost one too many times. In a regular NHL game, the referees usually replace the puck several times, but only once in NHL history has one puck been used for an entire game. On November 10, 1979, the Los Angeles Kings and the Minnesota North Stars played the whole game with just one puck. The puck, which is now on display in the Hockey Hall of Fame, never left the ice surface until the final buzzer sounded, despite a few missing chunks. In the early days of the NHL, pucks were not as readily available as they are today. For most games, only two pucks were used, one for the game and one for emergencies. If a puck flew into the crowd, fans had to throw it back onto the ice or face the wrath of arena security. After many altercations with fans, the league made it a rule to keep more than just two pucks at the arena.

255. **Only three coaches in the history of the game have led their teams to five or more Stanley Cup titles; name them.**

Answer: Scotty Bowman coached three different teams (Montréal, Pittsburgh and Detroit) to nine Stanley Cups; Hector "Toe" Blake led the Montréal Canadiens to eight Stanley Cups; and the Toronto Maple Leafs head coach Hap Day led his Leafs to five Cups.

256. **How was the winner of the second-longest game in NHL history (Boston Bruins versus Toronto Maple Leafs, 1933) almost decided when it went into the sixth overtime period?**

Answer: During the 1933 playoff semifinals between the Boston Bruins and the Toronto Maple Leafs, one of the strangest events in hockey history occurred. In the last game of the series, both teams battled to a scoreless tie at the end of regulation time. Into overtime, the two teams continued their defensive battle into the night, and after five overtime periods, the game was still scoreless. Both goaltenders refused to give any ground, keeping their teams in the game with some spectacular saves. Annoyed at the length of the game, someone representing the league suggested that both teams should just flip a coin to decide the winner. The referees agreed, and soon the coaches followed suit. Heads, you play for the Stanley Cup; tails, you lose and are soon playing golf. However, as soon as the exhausted but dedicated fans realized what was about to happen, they began to boo so loudly that the two teams had to abandon their coin-toss plans for fear that a riot would erupt. With reluctance, the two exhausted teams skated back out onto the ice to continue the game. The end finally came in the sixth overtime period when the Leafs Ken Doraty scored the series winner, to the great relief of everyone in the building.

257. Who was the first American-born player to be selected first overall in the NHL Entry Draft?

Answer: The Minnesota North Stars used their number one pick in 1983 to select Brian Lawton from New Jersey.

258. What NHL team has this saying posted in their dressing room, "to you from failing hands we throw the torch; be yours to hold it high"?

Answer: Dick Irvin Sr. had these famous words from poet John McCrae's poem "In Flanders Fields" inscribed on the walls of the Montréal Canadiens dressing room.

259. Who did the Montréal Canadiens waste their number one pick on in the 1980 NHL Entry Draft?

Answer: The Canadiens used their number one pick to select the highly recommended Doug Wickenheiser. After just four incomplete seasons with the Canadiens, he was happily traded to the St. Louis Blues. He bounced around the league for several years and finally retired in 1990, having played just 556 games. The Canadiens' other option that year was Denis Savard.

260. **What years did Don Cherry coach the Boston Bruins?**

Answer: From 1974 to 1979, Don Cherry proudly stood behind the bench of the Boston Bruins. He had a record of 231 wins, 105 losses and 64 ties.

Notes on Sources

Allen, Kevin, and Bob Duff. *Without Fear: Hockey's 50 Greatest Goaltenders*. Chicago: Triumph Books, 2002.

Batten, Jack. *The Leafs: An Anecdotal History of the Toronto Maple Leafs*. Toronto: Key Porter Books, 1994.

Brodeur, Denis, and Daniel Daignault. *Goalies: Guardians of the Net*. Montréal: Les Editions de L'Homme, 1995.

Carrier, Roch. *Our Life with the Rocket: The Maurice Richard Story*. Toronto: Viking Press, 2001.

Coleman, Charles L. *The Trail of the Stanley Cup*. Sherbrooke: Progressive Publications, 1969.

Diamond, Dan, ed. *Total NHL*. Toronto: Dan Diamond and Associates, 2003.

Diamond, Dan, and Eric Zweig. *Hockey's Glory Days: The 1950's and '60's*. Kansas City: Andrews McMeel Publishing, 2003.

Dryden, Ken. *The Game*. Toronto: Wiley Press, 2005.

Finnigan, Joan. *Old Scores, New Goals: The Story of the Ottawa Senators*. Kingston: Quarry Press, 1992.

Hornby, Lance. *Hockey's Greatest Moments*. Toronto: Key Porter Books, 2004.

Irvin, Dick. *The Habs: An Oral History from 1940–1980*. Toronto: McClelland & Stewart Inc., 1991.

Leonetti, Mike. *Maple Leaf Legends*. Vancouver: Raincoast Books, 2002.

Leonetti, Mike. *Canadiens Legends: Montréal's Hockey Heroes*. Vancouver: Raincoast Books, 2003.

Liss, Howard. *Goal! Hockey's Stanley Cup Playoffs*. New York: Delacorte Press, 1970.

McFarlane, Brian. *The Best of It Happened in Hockey*. Toronto: Stoddart Publishing, 1997.

McFarlane, Brian. *The Habs*. Toronto: Stoddart Press, 1996.

McFarlane, Brian. *The Original Six*. Toronto: Fenn Publishing, 2004.

Podnieks, Andrew, et al. *Kings of the Ice: A History of World Hockey*. Richmond Hill: NDE Publishing, 2002.

Podnieks, Andrew. *Return to Glory*. Toronto: ECW Press, 1995.

Richard, Maurice, and Fischler, Stan. *The Flying Frenchmen: Hockey's Greatest Dynasty*. New York: Hawthorn Books Inc., 1971.

Roxborough, Henry. *The Stanley Cup Story*. Toronto: Ryerson Press, 1964.

Turowetz, Allan, and Chrys Goyens. *Lions in Winter*. Scarborough: Prentice Hall, 1986.

Whitehead, Eric. *A Hockey Legend: Cyclone Taylor*. Markham: Paperjacks Ltd., 1982.

Wong, John Chi-Kit. *Lords of the Rinks*. Toronto: University of Toronto Press, 2005.

J. Alexander Poulton

J. Alexander Poulton is a writer and photographer and has been a genuine enthusiast of Canada's national pastime ever since seeing his first hockey game. His favourite memory was meeting the legendary gentleman hockey player Jean Béliveau, who in 1988 towered over the young awe-struck author.

He earned his B.A in English Literature from McGill University and his graduate diploma in Journalism from Concordia University. He has 12 other sports books to his credit, including books on hockey, soccer and baseball.